Chess Tactics
for the
Tournament Player

by
Grandmasters
Sam Palatnik and Lev Alburt

with
FM Roman Pelts as
Special Editorial Consultant

Library of Congress Catalog Card Number: 96-85855

2nd edition 1996.

ISBN 1-889323-02-0

10 9 8 7 6 5 4 3 2

Published by:
Chess Information & Research Center
P.O. Box 534
Gracie Station
New York, NY 10028-0005

For ordering information, see p. 248.

Distribution to the book trade in North America by:
W.W. Norton, 500 Fifth Avenue, New York, NY

Editor: Mark Ishee
Special Editorial Consultant: Roman Pelts
Translator: Eric Schiller
Typography: JM Productions and Sisu Solutions
Illustrator: Jami Anson
Cover: Mark Kostabi's painting, "The Ultimate Sacrifice"

Printed in the United States of America

Contents

Tactical Play

Decoy
Deflection
Obstruction / Blocking
Pin
Skewer

Clearing a Square
Clearing a Line
Clearing a Diagonal
Interference

Double Attack
Discovered Attack
Discovered Check
Double Check
X-Ray
In-Between Move

Foreword

Chess Tactics for the Tournament Player is the third volume in the "Comprehensive Chess Course" series. This book assumes that the reader is familiar with the rules of chess and with the basic concepts and tactical ideas outlined in the previous volumes.

The Comprehensive Chess Course originated in the former Soviet Union as a means of providing students with the most effective chess training. Thousands of masters and grandmasters were raised on this course of study. The Comprehensive Chess Course is based on the method of repeatedly presenting certain problems to students. The problems become progressively more difficult, combining new ideas with familiar ones, thereby broadening the student's knowledge and simultaneously reinforcing previously mastered material.

Like the two previous volumes, *Chess Tactics for the Tournament Player* is designed to be an ideal self-study guide. Virtually all the material is self-explanatory.

In the Introduction to *Comprehensive Chess Course, Volumes I and II*, we stated: "We estimate that the next portion of our course requires about 1,000 pages to provide the knowledge necessary to reach expert strength." The book you hold in your hands represents this next step in our ambitious attempt to translate and publish the entire course of study. The fourth book of this series is also in progress, and will discuss "Attacking the King."

We wish to take this opportunity to acknowledge our heavy debt to FM Roman Pelts, our special editorial consultant, who provided much of the material in this volume. In addition our editorial adviser Michael Vasilyev provided a lot of useful criticism and ideas for improvements for which we are grateful.

Important help was also received from Mark Ishee, while Lev Alburt's students Dr. Martin Katahn and Jan Cartier provided useful advice for how to make this book user-friendly for novices and non-masters. The authors are also grateful to Eugene N. Ruban for overall inspiration!

— GMs Sam Palatnik and Lev Alburt
New York City
October 10, 1995

Introduction

Chess Tactics for the Tournament Player is a textbook filled with instructive and thrilling examples of various kinds of tactical play. It is intended to benefit a wide range of players. Beginning players and tournament veterans alike will find interesting and instructive material.

In order to master tactics, forcing variations, and the art of making combinations, you must learn the art of calculation. In tournament play, you are not allowed to move the pieces freely at the board. In fact, once you touch a piece, you must move it, and you cannot change your mind and choose some other piece. So it is important to learn how to perform all necessary calculations in your head.

For that reason, it is best to try to use some parts of this book without a chessboard, relying on the diagrams alone. This can sometimes be a difficult task; therefore, from time to time you will want to set up the position on a chessboard or in a chessplaying computer program for assistance. But with some effort it is possible to work through most of the book without a chessboard, making it ideal for use while commuting on long or short journeys.

As you work through this book you will want to keep the following ideas in mind:

1. Each example contains a tactical device.

2. The solution to any diagram involves the realization of some concrete goal.

3. Each lesson focuses on a few specific ideas, though many of the examples employ a number of different tactical ideas.

Please also note that this is a textbook, not a workbook. The aim of *Chess Tactics for the Tournament Player* is to teach and explain the ideas upon which tactical play is based. The examples in lessons one through eight are intended to be read and studied, with a view to understanding how to create combinations. Each of these lessons is followed by 12 test positions called Exercises, which are designed to measure your understanding of the new material. You should try as hard as you can to solve the Exercises before looking up the solutions.

The following suggestions may be helpful in working though the Exercises:

1. In each example, try to find the solutions yourself, taking 10-15 minutes to discover the answer.

2. Don't move on to the next Exercise until you fully understand the current one. If you are not sure what the point is, study it further.

3. First try to read and analyze the moves without moving pieces on a chessboard.

4. Don't take anything for granted, especially when reading chess literature! Sometimes mistakes in published chess analysis go undetected for decades! Don't just blindly assume that we are correct. Check everything until you are satisfied that you understand the solution.

Lesson nine on "How to Calculate Variations" contains positions designed to sharpen your thinking skills. The goal of this chapter is not only to introduce the reader to the art of making accurate calculations but also to provide a solid foundation in correct chess thinking techniques upon which later books in this series will build.

— GMs Sam Palatnik and Lev Alburt

Lesson 1

Tactical Play

The subject of our book is tactics. But where should we begin? How can we convey to the reader the tactical ideas which exist in a sharp position?

The following example shows how a single misstep can be fatal:

Diagram 1

Kasparov – Polugaevsky, Moscow 1979

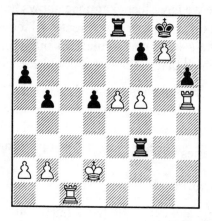

Black to move

1. ...	Rxe5?

This is a natural move, but it leads Black into a trap. Black had to play 1. ... Kxg7 2. Rg1+ Kh7 3. f6 Rg8 4. Rxh6+ with only a slightly better endgame for White.

2. f6!

This move simultaneously covers g7, attacks the rook at e5, threatens Rc8+ and the promotion of the g-pawn as well as Rxh6 and Rh8+. This makes it much more powerful than a mere double attack!

2. ...	Rf2+
3. Kd3	Rf3+
4. Kd4	Re4+
5. Kxd5	Re8
6. Rxh6	Rf5+
7. Kd4	Rf4+
8. Kc5	Re5+
9. Kb6	Re6+
10. Rc6	

And Black resigned because he has run out of checks.

The example we have just examined shows how important it is that each player properly evaluate all concrete threats. Although White's king was subject to many checks, he had properly calculated that in the end it could escape.

Experienced chessplayers know when to ask: "What does my opponent threaten?" Having identified the threats, they then determine if they are serious and must be defended against, or whether they can engage in more active operations.

What Is Tactical Play?

Most of the time a chess battle has a fairly quiet, maneuvering character. Each of the players acts, or at least *should* act, according to some plan which has a definite goal. Sometimes the plan is unambitious — for example, just regrouping pieces or occupying an open line. In other cases there are more profound ideas at work, such as an attack on the king, a queenside operation, a breakthrough in the center, etc. This sort of planning is generally referred to as chess *strategy*.

Tactics, on the other hand, are the battles that take place when the two players create threats against each other's men.

THREATS

Any attack against an enemy unit (including check) is an example of a *simple threat*, well-known to any beginner. Other simple threats involve lines which lead to favorable material exchanges. When we combine two or more simple threats, then we have a *complex threat*. For example, two powerful complex threats are the *double attack* and *discovered attack* (see Lesson 4).

The Importance of Making Threats

It is obvious that if you threaten to play a move that will win decisive material or checkmate the opponent, then the opponent must take measures to prevent it, no matter what his other plans might be. If threats follow one upon another, then the opponent has no time to realize a counter-plan. This is why the player with the more active position is considered to have the advantage (all else being equal), because the more active position makes it possible to create more threats, as in the following example:

Diagram 2
Kasparov – Palatnik, Daugavpils 1978

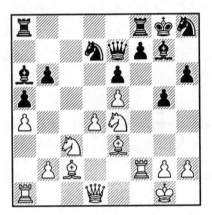

White to move

The knight on h8 is very badly placed, and it is hardly in a position to defend the king. In addition, Black's kingside pawn structure contains holes. White's pieces are well placed and ready for an assault on Black's king. Those three factors suggest that White might be able to exploit the situation by means of a sacrifice.

1. Bxg5!

The beginning of a decisive attack. An immediate 1. Qh5 is incorrect because Black has time to defend after 1. ... f5 2. Bxg5 Qf7.

1. ...	hxg5
2. Qh5	f5
3. Nxg5	Rf7!

The most obstinate defense, since other moves lose immediately, for example 3. ... Rfd8 4. Rxf5! and 3. ... Rfc8 4.Qh7+ Kf8 5. Nxe6+.

Diagram 3

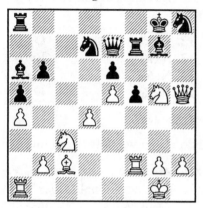

White to move

4. Bxf5!!

The sacrifice of a second bishop demolishes what is left of the defense by deflecting the Black pawn from e6, thereby permitting a knight invasion on d5.

4. ...	Rxf5

After 4. ... exf5, 5. Nd5 Qe8 6. e6 Rf6 7. Qh7+ Kf8 8. e7+ is decisive.

5. Rxf5	exf5
6. Nd5	Qe8
7. Qh7+	Kf8
8. Qxf5+	Kg8

Or 8. ... Nf7 9. Ne6+ Kg8 10.Qg6.

9. Qh7+	Kf8
10. Ra3!	

White will use the third rank to bring the rook into the attack, as the f1 square is controlled by Black.

10. ...	Rc8
11. Rf3+	Nf6
12. h3!	

This frees the h2-square for the king. Now Black is completely lost.

12. ...	Qg6
13. Rxf6+	Bxf6
14. Ne6+	Ke8
15. Nxf6+	

And Black resigned.

What conclusions can we draw from this example?

By creating a sequence of threat after threat, White simultaneously brought additional forces into the attack while Black had no choice but to use each valuable move to counter those threats. Black had no time to maneuver pieces, bring additional defensive resources into the battle or take any other measures to blunt White's attack.

Because White had so much firepower available on the kingside, it was possible to sacrifice pieces to open up the enemy position. In the end, the attack led to checkmate.

The key to White's success in this game, as in so many of the examples you will encounter in this book, is that *Black was unable to exploit the material superiority obtained as a result of White's sacrifices.* Too many of his pieces were not in a position to participate in the defense.

FORCED PLAY

A series of moves where the opponent has little or no choice of responses is called a *forcing variation*, as in the following example:

Diagram 4

Kasparov – Andersson, Tilburg 1981

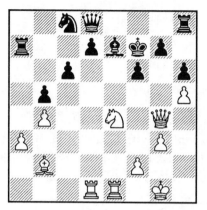

White to move

White has just achieved his strategic objective. All of his pieces are mobilized and occupy active attacking positions. The White forces swarm around the enemy king and are well coordinated. This is the foundation on which successful tactical operations are built.

1. Nxf6!!

The attempt to destroy the enemy defenses involves this flashy sacrifice of a knight.

1. ...   gxf6

This capture is forced, as 1. ... Bxf6 2. Qg6+ Kf8 3. Bxf6 gxf6 (3. ... Qxf6?? allows 4. Re8 mate) 4. Re6! and now 4. ... dxe6 is not available because of 5. Rxd8+, while there is otherwise no way to defend the f6-square. White's attack will thereby succeed.

2. Qg6+   Kf8
3. Bc1!

This sets up new threats and the attack grows.

3. ...   d5
4. Rd4

White adds more and more firepower to the attack.

| **4. ...** | **Nd6** |

Black is doing his best to defend.

| **5. Rg4** | **Nf7** |
| **6. Bxh6+!!** | |

Yet another tactical blow in the form of a sacrifice.

| **6. ...** | **Ke8** |

Black cannot capture with 6. ... Rxh6 because of 7. Qg8 mate, while 6. ... Nxh6 fails to 7. Qg7+. The rook at h8 cannot be defended, and the knight at h6 is also vulnerable.

| **7. Bg7** | |

Here Andersson resigned because on 7. ... Rg8 White plays 8.h6, and the advance of the pawn decides the game.

Now we are in a position to define exactly what we mean by "forcing variation": *A series of moves which alternate between a threat and a response to that threat.* The defending side cannot break this chain of alternating threats and defenses without losing material or allowing checkmate, until the forcing variation has come to an end.

Of course it would be wrong to assume that all activity on the chessboard consists of forcing variations. Without a doubt, most of the time chessplayers dream up forcing variations and sacrifices that never actually take place, often because the opponent takes measures to prevent them. Sometimes the tactical picture is as quiet as the strategic one, but all the same one must be able to calculate forcing variations to see how they might turn out, whether for good or bad.

The creation of forcing variations is crucial to a chessplayer's development. In a sharp position involving many forcing moves, variations with sacrifices may be worked out several moves ahead.

Gaining Time

In chess, time is measured in quantity of moves, known as *tempi* (the plural of the Italian *tempo*, meaning time). A move which does not accomplish anything is considered a waste of time. If we are able to force the opponent to make otherwise useless moves in order to counter our threats, and at the same time we are taking advantage of this to improve our position, then we are making threats which gain tempi. Such moves are considered to be made *with tempo*.

Making Threats with Gain of Time

Consider the following example where Black managed to win quickly by making two moves with tempo.

Diagram 5
Zita – Bronstein, Vienna 1957

Black to move

1. ...	c6!

Black has seen far in advance that a discovered check by ... Rf2+ will win if the d4 square can be controlled by a pawn on c5. He wins time by threatening the White rook twice. An immediate 1. ... c5 allows White a free move to play 2. Rd2 Rf2+ 3.Kc2.

2. Rd4

There is no choice. For example, 2. Rh5 Rf5+ or 2. Rxd6 Rxd6+ with a win of a rook in either case.

2. ...	**c5**
3. Rxd6	**Rf2+**

And White resigned.

Making an In-between Move

An *in-between move* [*Zwischenzug* in German] is a finesse that gains time or some other kind of advantage. See page 79 for a more detailed discussion.

Diagram 6

Alekhine – Flohr, Bled 1931

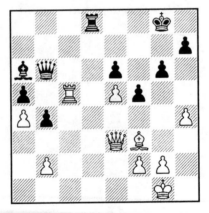

White to move

1. Rc8!

And Black resigned. After 1. ... Qxe3 White has the in-between move 2. Rxd8+ and then 3. fxe3 with an extra rook.

In the next diagram, we find a slight twist on the theme of the previous example, as the in-between move threatens mate.

Diagram 7
Stahlberg – Alekhine, Hamburg 1930

Black to move

1. ...	Rxf3!

And now if 2. Qxg5 then Black plays 2. ... Rxf2!! with the threat of 3. ... Rxf1 mate, and only then recaptures with 3. ... hxg5. So White resigned.

Making a Surprise Move

In a general chess sense, the term "in-between move" is used whenever an unexpected reply occurs instead of the anticipated move. This idea arises in the next position, where White did not recapture on b3 as Black had expected.

Diagram 8
Botvinnik – Menchik, Hastings 1930

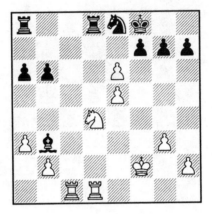

White to move

Instead, White played 1. e7+! and Black resigned, since 1. ... Kxe7 would be met by 2. Nc6+, finishing up an exchange with a winning position.

A single game can contain several unexpected moves as we see in the following position. Black expected White to play a routine recapture at h1, but like thunder on a sunny day, Tal unleashed:

Diagram 9

Tal – N. N., Stuttgart 1958

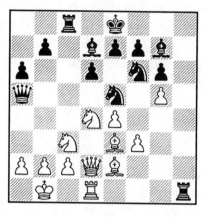

White to move

1. gxf6!

Now, in addition to the capture at h1, White has the threat of 2. fxg7 and 3. g8=Q mate.

1. ...	Rxd1+
2. Nxd1!!	

The quantity of threats has not diminished, since besides 3. fxg7, White has 3. Qxa5.

2. ...	Qxd2
3. fxg7!!	

Again there are a pair of threats, this time 4. g8=Q+ and 4. Bxd2.

3. ...	Be6
4. g8=Q+	Kd7
5. Qxc8+	Kxc8
6. Bxd2	**Black resigns**

The creation of forced play demands specific tactical skills which can be acquired via training. When studying lessons on tactics, pay close attention to both the means and the circumstances that give rise to forced play. Developing a sense for when circumstances are ripe will turn out to your advantage, since you will know how to evaluate forced play at the critical moment.

SACRIFICE

The acceptance of a sacrifice usually heats up the battle. Experienced chessplayers think long and hard before entering into a sacrifice, deeply calculating all possible results, knowing well that there may be unexpected resources (*in-between moves*) available to the opponent.

When you make a sacrifice, you should try to consider and evaluate the positions which arise after each move by each player. An error in calculation may lead to an incorrect sacrifice, and as a result the position may be lost instead of won.

If sacrifices are sometimes good and sometimes bad, then how can we talk about sacrifices in general?

In most of the examples in this book we can view the sacrifice as a seemingly *unprofitable exchange* — in the sense that the side which invests the material does not immediately receive an equal or greater amount of material in return.

Sacrifices can be either short-term or long-term investments. If the sacrifice leads to a rapid resolution of the game in our favor, then we consider it to be a *temporary sacrifice*.

Diagram 10

Bogolyubov – Capablanca, New York 1924

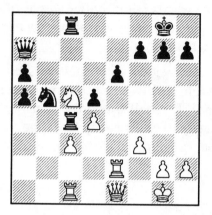

Black to move

| **1. ...** | **Nxd4!** |

A temporary sacrifice.

| **2. cxd4** | **R8xc5** |

A second temporary sacrifice.

3. dxc5

If 3. Rxc4, then 3. ... Rxc4 with three extra pawns for Black.

| **3. ...** | **Qxc5+** |

Followed by 4. ... Rxc1 with a decisive material advantage for Black.

Positional and Intuitive Sacrifices

All sacrifices are made with the goal of improving one's position. In addition to checkmate and the win of material, the improvement in the position can take many forms. For example, a sacrifice may create greater harmony among one's pieces, or give rise to an *initiative*. An initiative is a temporary advantage, during which the side with the initiative ties down the enemy pieces and creates threats.

Chessplayers sometimes sacrifice small amounts of material to obtain the initiative, and only later will objective analysis be able to determine whether the sacrifice was justified. In the case of a sacrifice to gain the initiative, calculating forcing variations is less important than intuition.

This book deals neither with intuitive sacrifices nor with sacrifices which result in obtaining purely positional advantages, since these fall within the domain of strategy, not tactics. Fortunately, there is a way to define the scope of our efforts: by concentrating on *combinations*, we confine our discussion to tactics alone.

COMBINATIONS

A combination is a forced variation usually involving a sacrifice which makes use of tactical devices to achieve a concrete goal.

By *concrete goal* we have in mind:

1. Checkmating the enemy king;

2. Achieving a material advantage;

3. Simplifying the position favorably; or

4. Escaping from a difficult position with the help of stalemate, perpetual check or repetition of moves.

These goals characterize most combinations.

Combinations occupy a special place among tactics. All accomplished chessplayers are familiar with them. Combinations add a particular flavor to the game, one which is appreciated by masters and beginners alike. The aesthetics, beauty and poetry of chess are inextricably bound to the idea of combinations.

Tactical Blows ("Shots")

Effective and unexpected moves that radically change the character of the battle are called *tactical blows* or, in chess slang, *shots*. Each combination consists of one or more tactical blows combined with forced play. For an experienced chessplayer the creation of a tactical blow may not be particularly difficult work because it is often a matter of technique which has already been acquired.

A tactical blow is the creative idea of a chessplayer in a concrete situation, and even the strongest players don't always take advantage of combinational possibilities. It is in part because of the creative, artistic foundations of a combination that chess is considered by many to belong to the arts as well as to sport and science.

Creating Combinations

A player who knows his craft can create ideas in a position by following correct rules and principles. This is possible because every chess position consists of objective factors.

It is not enough to know that combinations arise from forced moves; it is also necessary to show why the possibilities for combinations exist. For example, it is very seldom possible to mate the enemy king quickly if it is defended by pawn cover, has many pieces nearby for defense, and has plenty of room to maneuver. In such a position it makes no practical sense to search for a mating combination. But if the enemy king is confined and has few defenders and weak pawn cover, then experienced players will know that a mating combination may be possible. The same situation occurs with ideas for other types of combinations.

The conditions under which combinations can occur are limited. A combinational idea arises as a consequence of the tactical motifs which are present in a specific position.

Diagram 11
Kubbel, 1924

White to move

In this position there is a geometric motif based on the positions of the Black king and queen, and on the fact that the Black queen is undefended. This motif creates conditions for a skewer attack on the Black king and queen. There is only one square from which the White queen can use this geometric motif — a3. If the Black king were on a3, its movement would be very restricted. These observations form the logical chain on which the combination is based.

1. Qa3+!!   Kxa3

Or 1. ... Kb5 2. Qxe7

2. Nc2 mate

The *idea* of this combination is to decoy the Black king to a3.

If there is a combination in the position, three things must be present: *motif*, *idea*, and *technique*.

At first we become aware of the *motifs* that exist in the position. On the basis of this awareness we seek a combinative solution (the *idea*). Then we calculate the *technical part* — the forced play.

In remembering *motif, idea,* and *technique,* you might keep in mind the classic criteria for finding out whodunit: motive, opportunity and means!

The following example shows *motif, idea* and *technique* at work.

Diagram 12
Smyslov – Lilienthal, Leningrad 1941

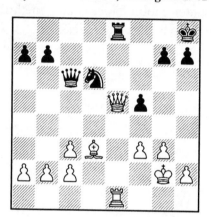

White to move

1. Qxd6

If 1. ... Qxd6 2. Rxe8+ leads to mate, and 1. ... Rxe1 loses to 2. Qf8 mate. After 1. ... Qc8 White has won a piece.

Here the *motif* of the combination is Black's back-row weakness. White notices this motif and searches for a way to remove Black's pieces from the back rank. The *idea* of the combination is deflection by removing the Black queen's guard on e8. The *technique* of calculating the forced variations considers all of Black's reasonable responses.

Having the idea alone does not make a combination. If the variation in which the tactical blow is delivered is not forced, then the combination will not succeed.

And where motifs are concerned, the situation is even more complicated. It sometimes happens that motifs are located deep within a position, and only experienced chessplayers can discover them. When a certain type of combination is familiar to you, then the motifs which characterize it are also familiar.

If on the other hand we are not familiar with a certain type of combination, then we won't recognize the motifs during the game and will pass up an opportunity to create a combination. A successful chessplayer must know as many motifs as possible. You will encounter motifs, ideas, and methods of creating forced play throughout our tactical lessons.

Lesson 2

Decoy, Deflection, Obstruction (Blocking), Pins, Skewers

This lesson features examples in which the main idea is a straightforward application of a single tactical device. You will become acquainted with the names of some of these devices and with the definition and usefulness of each.

We have selected positions from actual play to illustrate these ideas. Each one will focus on a single motif, and will allow you to learn about the motif without other factors interfering with your concentration. In later lessons we will examine still more motifs, and also consider how these interact and combine to produce successful forced variations.

Decoy

This tactical device forces an enemy piece onto a certain square by means of a sacrifice, threat, or other attack. Decoys are used together with other devices such as double attacks, discovered attacks, discovered checks, etc. A decoy is most effective when used against an enemy king.

Diagram 13
Reti – Tartakower, Vienna 1910

White to move

This is a classic example which every chessplayer should know by heart.

1. Qd8+!!

A brilliant queen sacrifice which has the effect of bringing the Black king to d8, where it will be subject to attack from rook and bishop simultaneously in the form of a *double check*.

A double check is the most powerful of the forcing devices. It allows the attacking side to bring two pieces into the attack simultaneously. Also, it is impossible to defend against two checks at once without moving the king, so the defending side usually has only a very limited number of replies available. This makes it easier to calculate all possible variations.

1. ...	**Kxd8**
2. Bg5++	**Kc7**

Or 2. ... Ke8 3. Rd8, a typical rook + bishop mate.

3. Bd8 mate

Diagram 14
Vidmar – Euwe, Carlsbad 1929

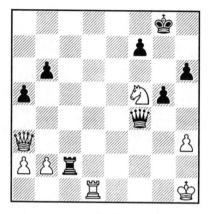

White to move

1. Qf8+!!

Luring the king to f8 to achieve a typical rook + knight mate. Black resigned. There is no escaping checkmate: 1. ... Kxf8 2. Rd8 mate or 1. ... Kh7 2. Qg7 mate.

Diagram 15
Nei – Petrosian, Moscow 1960

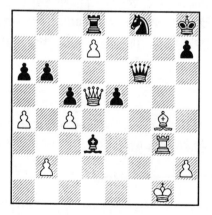

White to move

1. Qg8+

Black resigned. Checkmate follows on g8 in two moves.

Diagram 16

Geller – Dreev, New York 1990

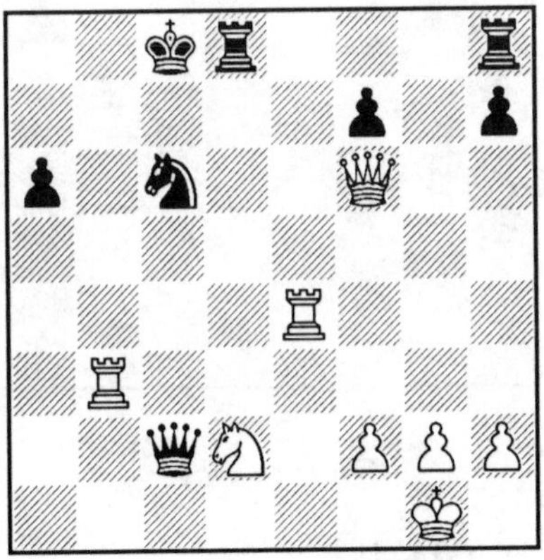

White to move

1. Qf5+!

Black resigned.

If 1. ... Rd7 White has 2. Re8+, and on 1. ... Kc7 White wins the Black queen with 2. Re7+. There are two ideas here — decoying the Black king or rook, and preparing a discovered attack using a geometric motif to exploit the unprotected queen on c2.

Deflection

Deflection is a tactical device used to remove a guarding piece or pawn from defending a square, line, or another piece.

Diagram 17

Instructive Example

White to move

Here the motif is the White pawn on the seventh rank. The Black rook guards the d8-square. With 1. Rg5! the Black rook is deflected from the d-file. On 1. ... Rxg5 there follows 2. d8=Q+ with a double attack.

Diagram 18

Spassky – Fischer, Argentina 1960

White to move

The Black queen defends the bishop at e7.

| **1. Re5!** | **Rd8** |

Counterattacking against the White queen. If 1. ... Qh4 then 2. Rxf8+! or 2. Qxh4, while 1. ... Bf6 runs into 2. Qd6!.

| **2. Qe4** | **Qh4** |
| **3. Rf4** | **Black resigns** |

Black's queen is forced to depart, leaving the bishop at e7 undefended.

The deflection and decoy ideas are most frequently encountered in conjunction with a sacrifice.

Diagram 19
Psakhis – Machulsky, Vilnius 1978

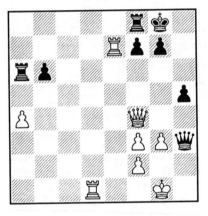

White to move

1. Rd8!

A deflection and a pin all rolled into one. Black resigned, since there is no defense to the threat of 2. Qxf7+. On 1. ... f6 or 1. ... f5, 2. Qc4+ wins easily.

Our next example shows how to drive a piece away from the defense of an important square.

Diagram 20
Paoli – Smyslov, Venice 1950

Black to move

1. ...	Rxc2!
2. Qxc2	Nf3+
3. Kf2	

If 3. Kh1 Qg3 wins.

3. ...	Qg3+

White resigned. On 4. Ke2 Black wins the queen with 4. ... Ned4+.

Obstruction (Blocking)

This tactical device limits the mobility of the enemy forces. In the majority of cases, the enemy king is the target. The most extreme and most famous example of obstruction is in the smothered mate and variations on that theme. Usually a series of checks is involved.

Diagram 21
Instructive example

White to move

1. Qc8+	**Qg8**

The obstruction tactic is executed. Now the Black king has no flight squares.

2. Qc3+	**Qg7+**
3. Qxg7 mate	

Diagram 22
Instructive Example

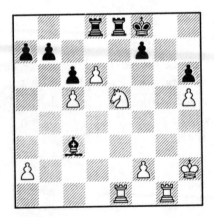

White to move

White exploits the fact that the Black king is blocked and cannot go to e7.

1. Nd7+	**Rxd7**
2. Rxe8+	**Kxe8**
3. Rg8 mate	

Diagram 23

Fischer – Benko, New York 1963-64

White to move

1. Rf6!

If 1. e5 then Black replies 1. ... f5!. So White uses an obstruction move to eliminate that defensive resource.

1. ...	**Kg8**
2. e5	**h6**
3. Ne2	**Black resigns**

The threat is 4. Rxd6, but if 3. ... Bxf6 then 4. Qxh6 wins, and if the Black knight moves then the f5-square is available for the White queen, followed by Qh7 mate.

Diagram 24
Lauders, 1903

White to move and mate in 3

Here the obstruction arises with the help of threats.

1. Qa7!

This threatens Qxc7 mate.

1. ...   Rxa7

Now the a7-square is blocked, and after

2. Kf7!

There is no defense to mate at g8.

Pinning

If you are already acquainted with this theme, you know that a pin is a tactical idea that prevents or discourages an enemy man from moving off a line lest it expose a comrade to capture or a key square to occupation. The pinned piece acts like a shield, which in both chess and life can be dangerous work.

An *absolute pin* arises when the shielded piece is the king. Then of course the pinned piece is not allowed to move away from the line along which it is pinned. Usually it can't move at all. *Relative pins* involve men covering pieces other than the king where the covered piece is more valuable than the pinned piece.

In the following famous example called "Legal's Mate," White breaks out of the relative pin by offering a queen sacrifice. Its acceptance leads to forced mate.

Diagram 25

Legal's Mate

White to move

1. Nxe5!	**Bxd1?**

Better to lose a pawn than get mated.

2. Bxf7+	**Ke7**
3. Nd5 mate	

For the moment, let's concentrate on the absolute pin, starting with the following example:

Diagram 26
Bronstein – N.N., Moscow 1953

White to move

White produced the following brilliancy:

1. Rd8+!!

Decoy.

1. ...   Kxd8

Now Black's Nf6 is pinned.

2. Qxe4

White wins the queen.

Diagram 27
Evans – Bisguier, U.S. Championship 1957

White to move

Black is a pawn ahead but White has the better position, which he exploits with a combination based on a pin.

1. Qa3+   Qe7?

Loses immediately. Black can resist better with 1. ... Kg8 2. Bxh7+ (a discovered attack) and then 3. Rxe6 with a material advantage for White.

2. Bc6!!

Another discovered attack, but the important point is that the queen at e7 is pinned in both a relative (if 2. ... Qxa3, then 3. Rxe8 mate) and absolute sense (2. ... Qxe1+ is illegal).

Let's look at a few more examples of pins at work.

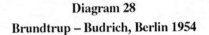

Diagram 28

Brundtrup – Budrich, Berlin 1954

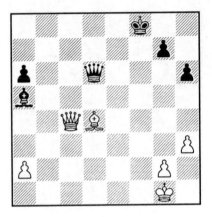

White to move

1. Bc5

The Black queen is pinned, but Black has a trick.

1. ...   Bb6

A cross-pin!

2. Qf4+!

Another exploitation of a pin, and this time it is final, because on the next move 3. Qxd6 will win an entire queen. If not for this check which wins the pinned Black queen, Black's cross-pin would have saved him.

Diagram 29

Ed. Lasker – Avalla, New York 1947

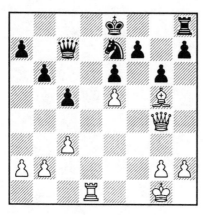

White to move

Black's king is stuck in the center, an unfortunate situation in most openings and middlegames. The White pieces are very active, and the dark squares are under the control of the White bishop. If you keep in mind that we are discussing pins here, and use a little creative thinking, you will be able to guess how the following combination works.

1. Qa4+	**Qc6**

Or 1. ... Kf8, in which case White has 2. Bh6+ Kg8 3. Qe8 mate, while 1. ... Nc6 fails to 2. Qxc6+ (deflection!) 2. ... Qxc6 3. Rd8 mate.

2. Rd8+!

A decoy that creates a pin.

2. ...	**Kxd8**
3. Qxc6	

Diagram 30

Kasparov – Browne, Banja Luka 1979

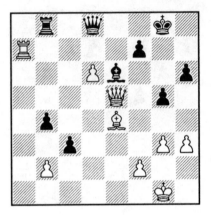

White to move

White has the advantage in the center and a rook on the seventh rank, but Black has some counterplay with his queenside pawns. White won by:

1. Bh7+!

First comes the decoy.

1. ...   Kxh7

Or 1. ... Kf8 2. Qh8 mate.

2. Qxe6

And Black resigned. The pawn on f7 is pinned and unprotectable. It is also the last defender of Black's king.

Skewers (the "shish-kabob" tactic)

The skewer is the opposite of a pin. It is a straight-line tactic attacking an enemy man, which if moved exposes the unit behind it to capture. In the following seemingly placid position, White combines the skewer with deflection to win immediately:

Diagram 31

Alexander – Cordingly, Surrey 1947

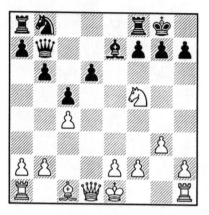

White to move

1. Qd5! Black resigns

A devastating skewer of Black's queen and rook at a8. The queen must be moved or protected.

The second player cannot try 1. ... Qxd5 because of 2. Nxe7+ Kh8 3. Nxd5 winning a piece in broad daylight. And if 1. ... Nc6, then 2. Qxc6 (deflection, but also winning is 2. Nxe7+) 2. ... Qxc6 3.Nxe7+ and 4. Nxc6. Finally, a clever attempt by Black to trap the queen via 1. ... Qc7 2. Qxa8 Nc6 is refuted by 3. Qxc6 Qxc6 4. Nxe7+ Kh8 5. Nxc6.

One of the most common skewers is when a queen gets skewered on an open central file with an unprotected rook on its own back rank:

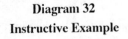

Diagram 32
Instructive Example

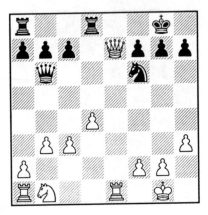

Black to move

1. ...	Re8

And Black wins. White saw a chance to win a pawn by 1. Qe2xe7??, but Black's response skewers the queen at e7 and the hanging rook on e1. Black's key piece here is the knight on f6, preventing White from playing 2. Qxe8+ and mate next move.

Exercises

1

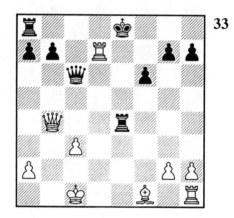

33

White to move

2

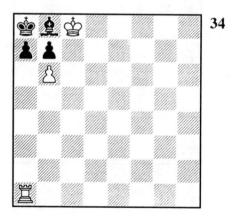

34

White to move and mate in 2

3

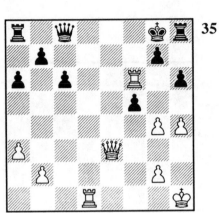

35

White to move

4

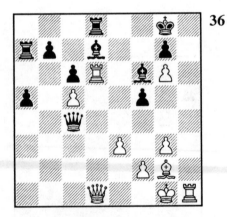

36

White to move

5

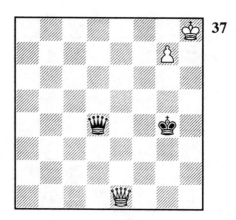

White to move

6

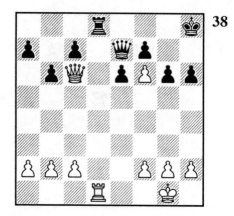

White to move

7

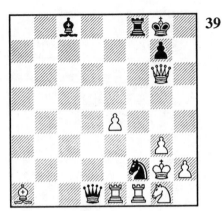

39

Black to move

8

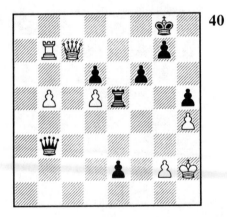

40

Black to move

9

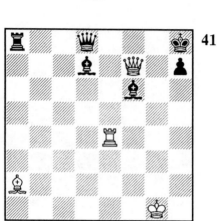

41

White to move

10

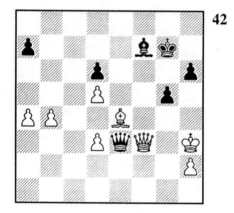

42

Black to move

11

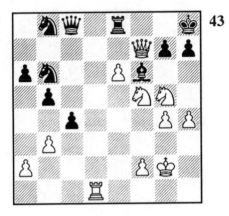

43

White to move

12

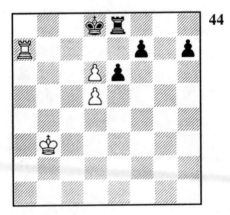

44

White to move
Hint: an obstruction idea is involved.

Solutions

1. Chiburdanidze-Andreyeva, Tbilisi 1973: 1. Re7+! (Best. 1. Rd4 saves the extra piece, but after 1. ... Rxd4 2. Qxd4 Rd8 3. Qe3+ Kf8 White has problems with his development.) 1. ... Rxe7 2. Bb5! picks up the queen.

2. Problem by Paul Morphy: 1. Ra6! and mate on the next move (deflection by means of *Zugzwang*).

3. Steinitz-N.N., London 1861: 1. Rd8+ (deflection) 1. ... Qxd8 (if 1. ... Kh7 2. Rxh6+ gxh6 3. Qe7+ Kg6 4. h5 mate) 2. Qe6+ Kh7 3. Rxh6+ (deflects g7 pawn) 3. ... gxh6 4. Qf7 mate.

4. Instructive Example: 1. Bd5+ (obstruction) 1. ... cxd5 2. Rh8+ (decoy) 2. ... Kxh8 3. Qh5+ Kg8 4. Qh7+ Kf8 5. Rxf6+ and mates.

5. Instructive Example: 1. Qg1+! Qxg1 2. g8=Q+ (skewer) winning.

6. Paglilla-Carbone, Argentina 1985: 1. Qa8! Rxa8 2. fxe7 wins.

7. Instructive Example: 1. ... Bh3+! 2. Nxh3 Qf3+ 3. Kg1 Qh1 mate.

8. Tolush-Keres, USSR 1939: 1. ... Qg3+! (a typical decoying idea with the goal of queening a pawn with check) 2. Kxg3 e1=Q+ wins.

9. Instructive Example: 1. Re8+! (obstruction and decoying).

10. Larsen-Spassky, Linares 1981: 1. ... g4+ (decoy) 2. Kxg4 Bh5+ 3. Kxh5 Qg5 mate.

11. Tal-Portisch, Biel 1976: 1. Nh6! (threatening smothered mate with 2. Qg8+) 1. ... gxh6 2. Qxh7 mate.

12. Instructive example: 1. d7! Re7 2. d6 Rxd7 3. Ra8 mate!

Lesson 3

Clearance and Interference

Square Clearance

The goal of this type of combination is the freeing of a square which is needed by another one of your pieces. Our first example comes from Alekhine:

Diagram 45

Alekhine – N.N.

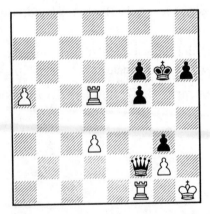

White to move

Can White capture the Black queen? At first glance this seems to lose, because after capturing the queen the Black pawn gets to f2 and there is apparently no way to prevent it from reaching the queening square. But the World Champion saw more deeply into the position!

1. Rxf2!	**gxf2**
2. Rxf5!!	**Kxf5**
3. g4+!	

The pawn advances with check and frees up the g2-square for use by the king, which can then handle the advanced pawn:

3. ...	**Kxg4**
4. Kg2	

And now it is Black who must give up, because White's a-pawn will soon become a new queen.

Here is another lesson from a World Champion:

Diagram 46

Bogolyubov – Capablanca, Bad Kissingen 1928

Black to move

To free the e4-square for his pawn, Black played ...

1. ...	**Nc5+!**

And White resigned, since the next move is 2. ... e4 mate.

Diagram 47

Bronstein – Medina, Göteborg 1955

White to move

Here a simple pawn move decides matters:

1. d6!

Black resigned, seeing what was just over the horizon: 2. Nd5! and the queen is trapped.

Diagram 48

Smyslov – Szabo, Hastings 1954-55

White to move

1. c6

This threatens both 2. Nc5+ picking off the bishop at b3, and 2. c7 winning the knight.

1. ...	exf4+
2. Kxf4	

and in a few moves Black resigned.

Clearing a Line

In combinations which are designed to clear a line, a piece or a pawn stationed along the line is sacrificed in order to set up a decisive blow.

Diagram 49

Fischer – Di Camillo, USA 1956

White to move

1. Bc7!

This frees the e-file and may also open up the d-file. If 1. ... Qxc7 then 2. d8=Q+, and if 1. ... Rxc7 then 2. Re8+! wins.

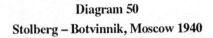

Diagram 50

Stolberg – Botvinnik, Moscow 1940

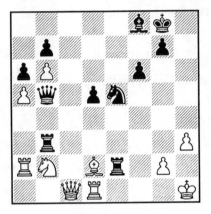

Black to move

1. ...	Rxh3+!
2. gxh3	d4!

Opening the diagonal for a check at d5 to be followed by mate at g2, so White resigned.

Diagram 51

Tal – N.N., Holland 1976

White to move

All of White's forces are swarming toward the kingside, where the enemy monarch is located. Is there a decisive breakthough here?

1. Rxc4!

This opens the b1-h7 diagonal.

1. ...   **bxc4**
2. Rf5!!

Threatening Rh5+. Black resigned — if 2....gf, White wins with 3.Qxf5+ Kh8 4.Qh5+ Kg8 5.Qg6+ and 6.Qg7 mate.

Diagram 52
Karpov – Csom, Bad Lauterberg 1977

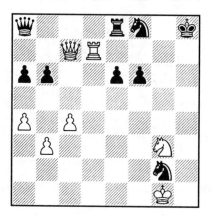

White to move

1. Nf5!   **Black resigns**

The knight opens the path to the h2 square for the queen. If 1. ... Nxd7 then 2. Qh2+! Kg8 3. Qg3+ and 4. Qg7 mate. On the other hand, 1. ... exf5 runs into a similar plan after 2. Qh2+ Kg8 3. Qg3+ Kh8 4. Qg7 mate. Black can attempt to contest the diagonal with 1. ... Qb8, but then White just carves another path with 2. Rh7+! Nxh7 3. Qg7 mate.

Diagram 53
Instructive Example

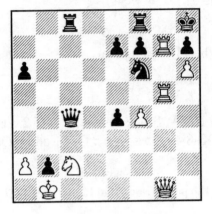

White to move

1. Rc5!	Qxc5
2. Rxh7+	

Now the g-file is clear.

and 3. Qg7 mate

Now for some examples of clearing a diagonal.

Diagram 54
Instructive Example

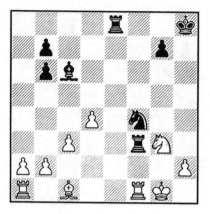

Black to move

If it weren't for the rook at f3, Black could deliver checkmate with 1. ... Nh3. So how do we resolve the situation? This way:

| 1. ... | **Rf2!** |

The threat is 2. ... Nh3.

2. Bxf4

If the king tries to run away he gets caught: 2. Kxf2 Nh3 mate. On 2. Rxf2 Black has 2. ... Re1+ 3. Rf1 Nh3 mate.

2. ...	**Rg2+**
3. Kh1	**Rxg3+**
4. Rf3	**Bxf3 mate**

Diagram 55
Instructive Example

White to move

In this position White's bishop is in the way. If it were magically removed from the board, then Qg6 would be mate. We must get the bishop out of the way without giving Black time to defend.

1. Bb7!

Black cannot simultaneously deal with the threat to the queen and the threat of mate at g6.

Interference

You can use the idea of interference to disrupt the harmonious interaction of the defensive forces. Often the goal of this tactic is to take control of a critical square. The interference device is used to insure that the enemy cannot maintain control of the critical square, file, rank or diagonal.

Diagram 56
Reti-Bogolyubov, New York 1924

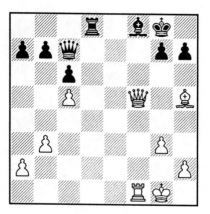

White to move

White uses the interference tactic to disrupt the defenses along the back rank.

1. Bf7+   Kh8
2. Be8!!

The game comes to an unexpected conclusion. The threat of Q(x)f8+ cannot be countered.

Diagram 57
Euwe – Thomas, Hastings 1934-35

White to move

The game lasted just one more move:

1. Bd5!   **Black resigns**

There is no way out, since 1. ... Rxf2 loses to 2. Qg8 mate and
1. ... Qxd5 allows 2. Rxf8+. This example combines discovered
attack with defense (stopping potential counterplay against g2).

Diagram 58
Instructive example

Black to move

After 1. ... Nh3+! the communication between White's queen and the h2-square is disrupted (interference). To avoid immediate checkmate White must play 2. Qxh3 Bxh3, after which Black has a big material advantage.

Diagram 59

A study by Heyecek, 1930

White to move

White wins in this study by not allowing the Black pawn to advance to e4, in which case the Black bishop would guard the queening square h8.

1. Ba7!

Black cannot capture, because then the pawn at h6 waltzes into the queening square. So the bishop hides on the long diagonal, praying for the opportunity to move his pawn.

1. ...	Ba1
2. Kb1	Bc3
3. Kc2	Ba1
4. Bd4!!	

A classic example of interference. If Black captures with 4. ... exd4 then White plants the king on d3, and the pawn will never advance. So ...

4. ...	Bxd4
5. Kd3	Ba1
6. Ke4	

And the h-pawn promotes.

Exercises

1

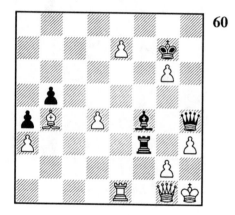

60

White to move

2

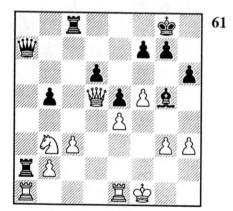

61

Black to move

3

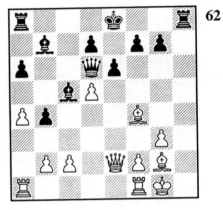

62

Black to move

4

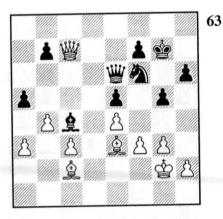

63

Black to move

5

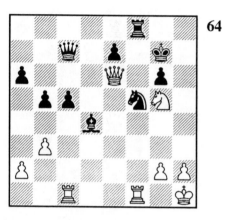

64

White to move

6

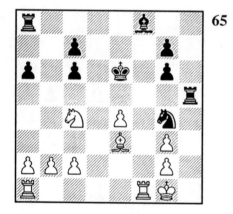

65

Black to move

7

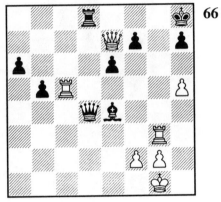

66

White to move

8

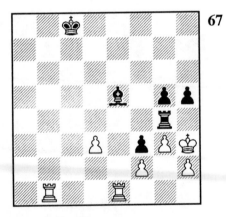

67

Black to move

9

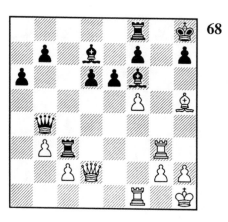

68

White to move

10

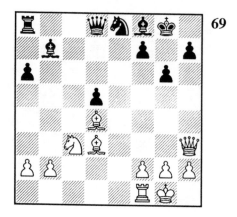

69

White to move

11

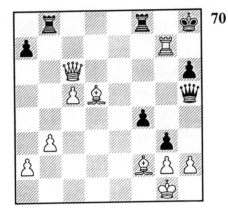

70

White to move

12

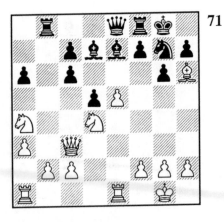

71

White to move

Solutions

1. Spassky-Korchnoi, Moscow, 1955: Black's threat is 1. ... Rxh3+, for example after 1. e8=Q?, but 1. Qh2!! and Black resigns. 1. ... Bxh2 (interference) 2. e8=Q and Black is dead.

2. Unzicker-Fischer, Varna, 1962: 1. ... Rxc3!! White resigns. 2. bxc3 open the second rank for 2. ... Qf2 mate.

3. Gutop-Roshal, Moscow, 1963: 1. ... Qxd5!! White resigns. After 2. Bxd5 Bxd5 mate is inevitable on the open white diagonal.

4. U.Andersson-Hartston, Hastings, 1972-73: 1. ... Qh3+!! White resigns since after 2. Kxh3 Bf1 with mate on the diagonal f1-h3; and if instead 2. Kf2 (or 2. Kg1) 2. ... Qf1 mate.

5. Tal-Parma, Bled, 1961: 1. Qxf5! Black resigns (1. ... Rxf5 and 1. ... gxf5 are both answered by the fork 2. Ne6+).

6. Dely-Kerkoff, Sombor, 1966: 1. ... Bc5!! White resigns (on 2. Bxc5 Rah8 is killing).

7. Eliskases-Hoetzl, Graz 1931: 1.Rd5! wins.

8. Instructive Example: 1. ... Rh4+ 2. gxh4 g4 mate.

9. Tal-Platonov, Dubna 1973: 1. Qh6 Rxg3 2. Bg6!! Rxg6 3. fxg6 wins.

10. Malesic-Misic, Yugoslavia 1965: 1.Bxg6! and Black resigned.

11. Ftacnik-Georgiev, Groningen 1977: 1. Rg8+! Rxg8 2. Bd4+ Rg7 3. Bxg7+ Kxg7 4. Qc7+ Kf6 5. Qxf4+ Qf5 6. Qd6+! Kg7 7. Qxg3+ and 8. Qxb8.

12. Instructive Example: 1. Bxg7 Kxg7 2. e6! fxe6 3. Nf5++ and mate.

Lesson 4

Double / Discovered Attack and X-Ray

Double Attack

A *double attack is a single move which makes two separate threats at the same time.* You may sometimes hear that the terms fork and double attack have different meanings, but in practice they are interchangeable. The knight is especially well-suited to attacking two pieces at once, and the knight fork has been known to trip up even the most experienced players. For example:

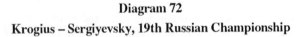

Diagram 72
Krogius – Sergiyevsky, 19th Russian Championship

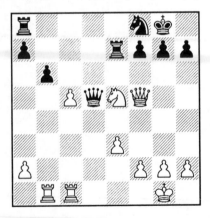

1. Ng6!!

Black resigned. If the queen moves Black loses the exchange, but after 1. ... Qxf5 2. Nxe7+ Kh8 3. Nxf5 White has an extra rook, and after 1. ... Rd7 2. Ne7+ White wins a queen for a knight.

The key square here is e7. We can follow the construction of the combination this way: the Black queen is undefended; White wants to capture the enemy queen, but can't because the knight is in the way. There is also a relationship between the queen at d5 and the king on g8, which can be exploited by moving the knight to e7, which just happens to be conveniently occupied by an enemy rook. These circumstances allow White to play the combination and win.

Discovered Attack

A *discovered attack* involves three pieces which are positioned on the same line (rank, diagonal or file). If the obstructing piece can move with a powerful threat (such as a check) then the piece it uncovers is free to capture an enemy piece.

Diagram 73
Ghitescu – Fischer, Leipzig 1960

White made a major oversight here, playing 1. dxc5. Fischer replied 1. ... Bxh2+! and White resigned, because after White deals with the check, Black will capture the unprotected White queen at d3.

Diagram 74

Beisdorf – Lipola, Helsinki 1957

1. Qxc8+! (decoy) forced Black to resign, since the opening of the first rank after 1. ... Kxc8 2. Bh3+ (discovered attack) will lead to the win of the Black queen at h1, and in the end White will have an extra bishop.

Diagram 75

Fischer – Spassky, World Championship 1972

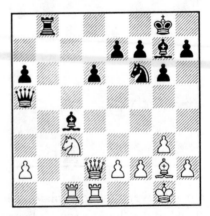

Here Black played

1. ...	**Nd7?**

And White answered

2. Nd5!	**Qxd2**
3. Nxe7+	**Kf8**
4. Rxd2	**Kxe7**
5. Rxc4	

And White won a pawn and now has an extra exchange, which was sufficient to win.

Diagram 76
Trifunovic – Aaron, Beverwijk 1962

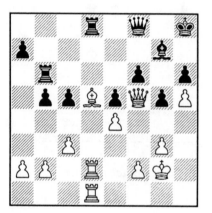

1. Bg8!!

The threat of Qh7 mate forces Black to play 1. ... Qxg8, but now the open line comes into play, and White continues 2. Rxd8, which also sets up a pin on the enemy queen. So Black played 2. ... Bf8, but after 3. Rd2-d7 there is no defense to the threat of 4. Rxf8! Qxf8 5. Qh7 mate.

Discovered Check

Discovered check is a form of discovered attack where the enemy piece involved is the king. The piece that moves out of the way to allow the check to be delivered can be anything but the queen. The piece which delivers the check can be queen, rook or bishop.

Discovered check is a very powerful weapon. Because the opponent must respond to the check, the piece that moves away to provide the discovery can safely do almost anything it pleases.

Diagram 77

Donner – Keres, Zurich 1959

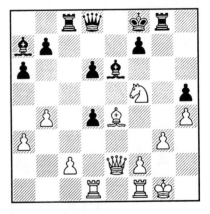

Black to move

1. ...　　　　　　　　　　**Bxf5!**

White resigned, since after 2. Bxf5 Rxg3+ 3. fxg3 there is the discovered check 3. ... d3+ winning the queen.

Diagram 78

Short – Ludgate, England 1977

White to move

This example shows the power of the deeply advanced pawn:
1.Qg7+! Qxg7 2. e7+ and White wins.

Diagram 79

Anderssen – Lange, Breslau 1859

Black to move

A discovered check is a nasty piece of work, and its brutal
effect can be seen in this ancient game. Black played 1. ... h5!!
and White was forced to give up, since there is no defense after

2. Rxg5 hxg4+ 3. Rh5 Rxh5 mate, and 2. gxh5 Qxf5 also leaves White with no defense against checkmate.

To get the full effect from a discovered check, you must find the best square for the piece that is getting out of the way of the checking piece. Sometimes this is a retreat, as in the following case:

Diagram 80

Cooper – Boll, Vulca 1881

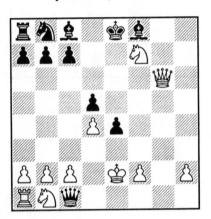

White to move

The best move here is to move backwards to the square where the knight will be protected by the pawn:

1. Ne5+	**Ke7**

If 1. ... Kd8, then 2. Qf6+ Be7 3. Qh8+ Bf8 4. Qxf8 mate.

2. Qf7+	**Kd6**
3. Qf6+	**Be6**
4. Qxf8 mate	

You don't need a lot of pieces to pull off a powerful discovered check. Here is an example with just four pieces on the board.

Diagram 81

V. Speckman, 1971

White to mate in two

White mates in two with 1. Kf6+ and there is no escape for Black. If 1. ... Kf8 2. Qc8 mate and 1. ... Kh8 gets mated by 2. Qg7 mate.

Sometimes the discovery can be spectacular, as in the following example which displays the technique known as the "windmill."

Diagram 82
Instructive Example

1. Rxg7+ Kh8 2. Rxf7+ Kg8 3. Rg7+ Kh8 4. Rxd7+ Kg8 5. Rg7+ Kh8 6. Rxc7+ Kg8 7. Rg7+ Kh8 8. Rxb7+ Kg8 9. Rg7+ Kh8 10. Ra7+ Kg8 11. Rxa8

Diagram 83

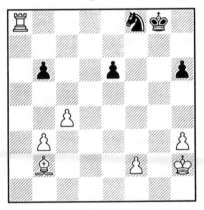

Comparing the two diagrams, we notice that most of the remaining pieces (except for the White rook) are in the same positions in which they started. But the Black king has watched most of his army disappear!

Double Check

Double check is a form of discovered check. In a double check the piece which moves out of the way of the main checking piece also gives check. Notice that there can be no double check unless one of the checks is a discovered check (try to construct one and you'll soon see why). There is only one defense to a double check—the withdrawal of the king. A double check takes place on a file, diagonal or rank, using a battery (two pieces working together). A double check is such a powerful weapon that it often brings the game to a swift and victorious conclusion.

Steinitz-Meitner, Vienna 1860

1.e4 e5 2.Nf3 Nc6 3.d4 exd4 4.Bc4 Bc5 5.0-0 Nf6 6.e5 d5 7.exf6 dxc4 8.Re1+ Be6 9.Ng5 Qd5 10.Nc3 Qf5 11.g4 Qxf6 12.Nd5 Qd8 13.Rxe6+ fxe6 14.Nxe6 Qd7 15.Qe2 Be7 16.Ndxc7+ Kf7 17.Qxc4 Ne5 18.Qb3 Qd6 19.f4 Nxg4

Diagram 84

20.Ng5++ Kg6 21.Qd3+ Kh5 (21. ... Kf6 22. Ne4+) **22.Qh3+ Kg6 23.Qxg4 Qb6** (23. ... h5 24. f5+ Kf6 25. Ne4+ Kf7 26. Nxd6+) **24.Nge6+ Kf6 25.Qg5+ Kf7 26.Qxg7 mate**

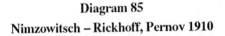

Diagram 85

Nimzowitsch – Rickhoff, Pernov 1910

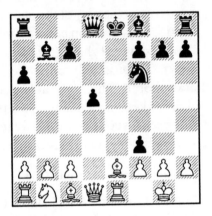

White to move

1.Bb5++ is a double check and mate! That's about as powerful a move as you can make.

Zaitsev-Karpov, Leningrad 1966

1. e4	e5
2. Nf3	Nf6
3. d4	Nxe4
4. Bd3	d5
5. Nxe5	Nd7
6. Nxf7	Qe7

It would be interesting to accept the gift with 6. ... Kxf7 because of 7. Qh5+; for example, 7. ... Kg8 8. Qxd5 mate, or 7. ... g6 8. Qxd5+ and 9. Qxe4 with two extra pawns, but after 7. ... Ke6 or 7. ... Ke7 Black has a chance to save his material advantage. Karpov prefers the initiative.

7. Nxh8	Nc3+

A discovered check!

8. Kd2	Nxd1
9. Re1	

Pinning.

9. ...	Nxf2
10. Bxh7	Ne4+
11. Rxe4!	dxe4
12. Bg6+	Kd8
13. Nf7+	

Diagram 86

13. ...	Ke8
14. Nd6+	Kd8
15. Nf7+	

The double check led to a draw by perpetual check!

X-Ray

This term is taken from the realm of chess composition. An X-ray is a a technique where a piece "looks through" an enemy piece toward a target, usually a mating square. This is very much like a pin, except that instead of being pinned to a piece, an enemy unit is pinned to a square instead.

In the next position, White has a big threat: 1. Qh7+ Kf8 2. Qxg7+!! Kxg7 3. Ne6+ and mate follows at h8. Fortunately for Black, it is his turn to move. But is there a defense?

Diagram 87

Instructive Example

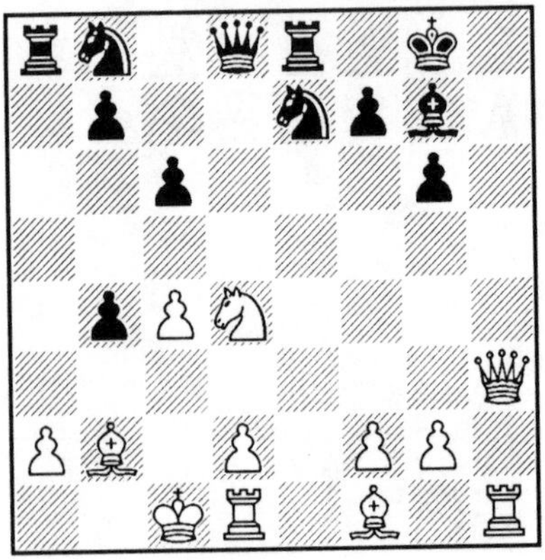

Black to move

1. ...   Bxd4

This takes care of the main threat, but White has prepared a surprising reply.

2. Qh8+

This blow is possible because of the x-ray threat at h8.

2. ...   Bxh8
3. Rxh8 mate

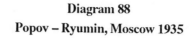

Diagram 88
Popov – Ryumin, Moscow 1935

White has just retreated his queen to d2, and the X-ray *motif* strikes with devastating effect. The *idea* of this blow involves both decoying and double check.

1. ...	Rxf3!
2. Bxf3	Qxf3+!!
3. Kxf3	Nxd4++!
4. Kg4	Bc8+
5. Kh4	Nf3 mate

In-between Move

When it comes to surprises, the most frequent one at the chessboard is the in-between move, commonly referred to by its rather unwieldy German name *Zwischenzug*. This takes place when one side is in the middle of a tactical operation, expecting a particular reply (usually a recapture), but the opponent suddenly unleashes a powerful move which does not directly address the threat.

Diagram 89

Rossetto – Sherwin, Portoroz 1958

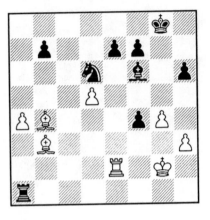

1. ...	Rb1
2. Bxd6	

White only reckoned on the recapture 2....exd6 here. But Black has an in-between move.

2. ...	f3+!

White resigned, since after 3. Kxf3 Rxb3+ and only then 4. ... exd6 Black wins too much material.

An in-between move is especially hard to predict in advance when it doesn't involve a check.

Diagram 90
Lilienthal – Panov, Moscow 1949

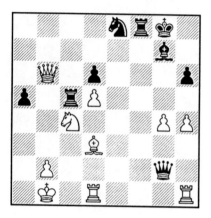

Black to move

| 1. ... | Rxc4! |

The rook is taboo, because of 2. ... Rf2.

| 2. Rhg1 | Rb4! |
| 3. Qxb4 | Qxg1! |

This in-between move allows Black to emerge from the battle with an extra piece in hand.

| 4. Bh7+ | Kh8! |

Black can't play 4. ... Kxh7 because of 5. Qe4+ and then 6. Rxg1.

| 5. Rxg1 | axb4 |

And Black eventually won.

Diagram 91

Study by Otten

White to move

1. a5	Bf8
2. Kd5	Bh6
3. g5+!	

This winning idea involves an in-between move with check.

3. ...	Bxg5

3. ... Kxg5 4. a6 and the Black king blocks his bishop.

4. Ke4!	Bh4
5. Kf3	

And the pawn promotes to a queen.

Diagram 92
Gruenfeld – Alekhine, Carlsbad 1923

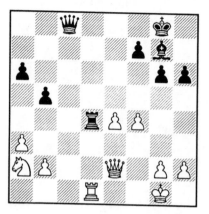

Black to move

The game continued ...

1. ...	Qc4!
2. Qxc4	Rxd1+
3. Qf1	Bd4+

... concluding with a final in-between move. White resigned.

In-between moves can pop up at any stage of the game. Here's proof:

In the Opening

Tartakower-Capablanca, New York 1924

1. e4	e5
2. f4	exf4
3. Be2	d5
4. exd5	Nf6
5. c4	c6
6. d4	Bb4+
7. Kf1	cxd5
8. Bxf4	dxc4
9. Bxb8	

White hopes to win a bishop after 9. ... Rxb8? 10. Qa4+, but:

Diagram 93

9. ...	Nd5!

This in-between move protects the bishop at b4 from the threat of Qa4+ while creating the threat of forking White's queen. And if White retreats the bishop with 10. Bf4, then 10. ... Qf6!. Black obtained a superior game and went on to win.

In the Middlegame

Diagram 94
Panov – Makogonov, Tbilisi 1937

White to move

Black expected White to recapture at e5, but there is a better move:

| 1. f7+! | Rxf7 |
| 2. Qxe5 | |

Now the a1-h8 diagonal is open, with winning threats.

2. ...	Kf8
3. Qg7+	Ke7
4. Bb4+	**Black resigns**

In the Endgame

Diagram 95
Sopkov – Moiseyev, USSR 1952

White to move

To reach this position, White captured a bishop at c5, and in return Black captured a bishop at g2, expecting the natural 1. Kxg2, in which case the reply 1. ... Bd5+ wins the knight at c6 with equality. But White played

1. Ne7!

And now Black had to resign, because the in-between move set up the deadly threat of 2. Bd4 mate, so there was no time to extricate the knight from g2.

Exercises

1

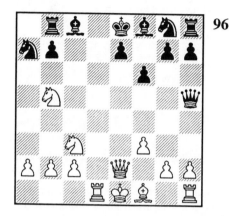

96

White played 1. Nd6+ and Black resigned. Why?

2

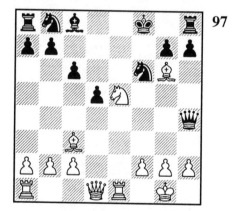

97

Black to move. He played 1. ... Na6.
But could he have taken the bishop at g6?

3

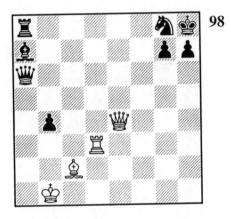

98

Find the best continuation assuming it is White to move,
and then do the same if Black is to move.

4

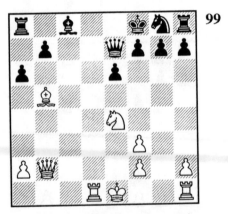

99

Black's last move was 1. ... a6.
Could White have responded 2. Qa3?

5

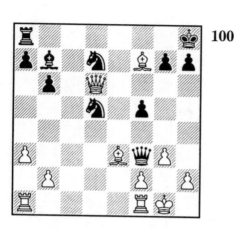

100

White played 1.Bh5.
How would you have replied if you were Black?

6

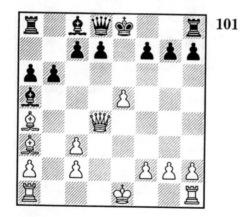

101

After 1. e6! Qf6 find the mate in 3 moves.

7

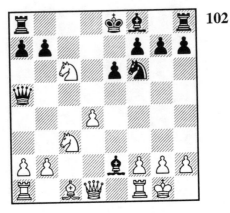

102

Black to move

8

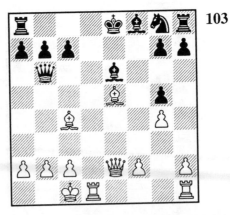

103

White to move

9

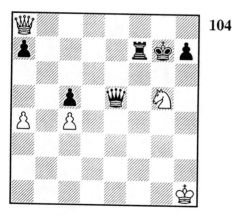

104

White to move

10

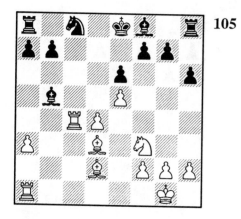

105

White to move

11

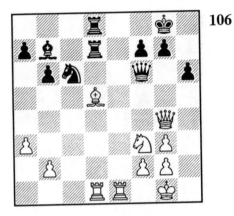

106

White to move

12

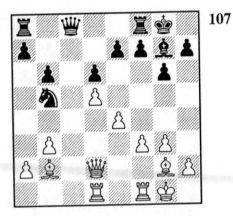

107

White to move

Solutions

1. Boleslavsky-Gurgenidze, USSR 1960: Black resigned because on 1. ... Kd8 or 1. ... Kd7 White has 2. Nxc8+ Kxc8 (2. ... Kc7 3. Nxa7 and White has a material advantage as well as an attack) 3. Qe6+ Kc7 4. Rd7+ Kc8 5. Rd6+ Kc7 6. Qd7 mate.

2. Smyslov-Kamyshov, USSR 1944: No, you can't afford to capture the bishop: 1. ... hxg6 fails to 2. Nxg6+ and after the king moves, White grabs the queen with 3. Nxh4.

3. Instructive Example: A. If it is White to move, the win is 1. Qxh7+! Kxh7 2. Rh3 mate; B. With Black to move, the tables are turned: 1. ... Qa1+! 2. Kxa1 Bd4++ 3. Kb1 Ra1 mate.

4. Euwe-Benitez, 1948: Yes, indeed. White plays 1. Qa3! to deflect the enemy queen from defending d8, and now 1. ... Qxa3? 2. Rd8+ Ke7 3. Re8 mate.

5. Utyaganov-Konovalov, USSR 1950: The correct continuation on 1. Bh5 is 1. ... Qg2+! 2. Kg2 Nf4++ 3. Kg1 Nh3 mate.

6. Alekhine-Forrester, 1923: 1. Bxd7 Kd8 2. Bc6+ Qxd4 3. e7 mate.

7. Perlis-Tartakower, Moscow 1907: 1. ... Qxc3! and now 2. Qxe2 Qxc6 or 2. bxc3 Bxd1 or finally 2. Qa4 Qc6 leaves Black with at least an extra piece.

8. Boleslavsky-Lilienthal, Leningrad 1941: 1. Bxc7!, for example 1. ... Qxc7 2. Qe6+ Ne7 3. Qf7 mate or 2. ... Qe7 3.Bb5 mate.

9. Petrosian-Simagin, Moscow 1956: 1. Qxh8+! (decoy) 1. ... Kxh8 2. Nxf7+ (fork) 2. ... Kg7 3. Nxe5 and White has a winning endgame.

10. Sveshnikov-Timman, Holland 1992: 1. Rxc8+ Rxc8 2. Bb5+ and White has won two pieces for the rook.

11. Kasparov-Karpov, Moscow 1985: 1. Qxd7! Rxd7 2. Re8+ Kh7 3. Be4+ g6 4. Rxd7 and here the two rooks are stronger than the queen.

12. Botvinnik-Golombek, Moscow 1956: 1. Bxg7 Kxg7 2. Rc1! Qd7 3. a4 Black resigns (on 3. ... Nc7 4. Qc3+ Black loses his knight).

Lesson 5

Destructive Combinations

We have seen a number of examples of attacking play involving a king that was exposed. Now we must turn our attention to the task of stripping away the defenses that usually protect the king. To that end we will study *destructive combinations* which are designed to remove the king's defenders.

To try to master the art of attack without understanding these destructive combinations is futile. If you are involved in an attack and pass up the opportunity to score the point by combinative means, you may find that there is no way to win the game, or that the game is prolonged because you failed to strike at the necessary moment. Destructive combinations can also emerge suddenly, as a consequence of mistakes made by you or by your opponent.

In the examples presented in this chapter, the attacker will destroy all or part of the defense by means of a sacrifice, which leads either to mate or to material advantage. But note that mate or the win of material is not always the goal of a destructive combination. Sometimes a destructive combination is made in order to gain attacking chances, to create practical problems for the opponent, or to improve the harmony of the pieces in the attack.

Seizing a Square

To illustrate the basic idea, let's consider a few examples where the enemy king is already vulnerable, and can be finished off by a simple combination by threatening a mate delivered on a weakened square. These combinations are often characterized by the sacrifice of a piece which is either under attack or is deliberately left *en prise*.

Diagram 108

Spielmann – Tartakower, Marienbad 1925

White to move

1. Qh6!

Here White sacrifices the rook which sits undefended at e1 in order to create an immediate and fatal threat of mate at g7.

1. ...	Qxe1+
2. Bf1	

Now Black could delay immediate defeat by 2. ... Qe3+, but the game continued ...

2. ...	Re8
3. Qg7 mate	

Diagram 109
Taimanov – Zhukhovitsky, USSR 1949

Black to move

White threatens both the black king and queen (Rd8+), but a surprising move follows.

| 1. ... | Ng4! |
| 2. g3 | |

The queen can't be captured because of the *smothered* mate at f2.

2. ...	Qc6+
3. Rg2	Nf2+
4. Kg1	Nxd1

And White resigned.

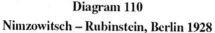

Diagram 110
Nimzowitsch – Rubinstein, Berlin 1928

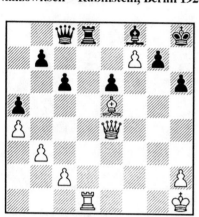

White to move

1. Qg6!

Black resigned, since there is no defense to the threat of Qxh6+. If 1. ... Rxd1+, then 2. Kg2 Rd2+ 3. Kh3 and Black has only one check left to give.

Now let's move on to actual destructive combinations. Here the enemy king is not exposed, so we have to do something to create the mating attack.

In the next example we would like to check the enemy king at b6, but that square is protected by a pawn. How do we demolish that protection, while maintaining the initiative?

Diagram 111
Averbakh – N.N., USSR 1954

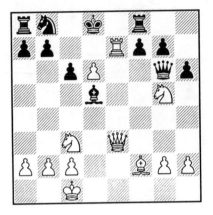

White to move and force mate

1. Qb6+!!

This takes control of b6 with decisive effect by sacrificing the queen to destroy the king's protection.

1. ...	axb6
2. Bb6+	Kc8
3. Rc7+	Kd8
4. Rxf7+!	Kc8

Or 4. ... Ke8 5. Re7 mate.

| 5. Rxf8+! | Kd7 |
| 6. Rd8 mate! | |

Diagram 112
Instructive Example

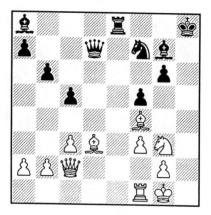

White to move

In this position White chose to regroup his forces.

1. Kf2??

But he was snared in a mating net after ...

    1. ...   **Bd4+!**

Taking control of d4.

    2. cxd4   **Qxd4+**

And after 3. Be3 comes 3. ... Qxe3 mate.

Breaking Down the Defense

In these combinations sacrifices are used to eliminate important defenders. As a result, the opponent is left without sufficient resources to hold off the attack or combat a specific threat.

Diagram 113
Instructive Example

White to move

1. Qxb8+!

Removing the defender of the c6 and d7 squares.

1. …   **Rxb8**
2. Bxb5 mate

Diagram 114
Instructive Example

White to move

The Black rook at d8 defends the eighth rank from the back rank mate with Re8+, but only for the moment.

> **1. Qxd8!+**   **Bxd8**
> **2. Re8 mate**

Diagram 115

Instructive example

White to move

Here the knight at e8 defends against the threat of mate at g7. So this knight must be eliminated.

> **1. Rxe8+!**   **Rxe8**
> **2. Qxg7 mate**

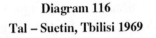

Diagram 116

Tal – Suetin, Tbilisi 1969

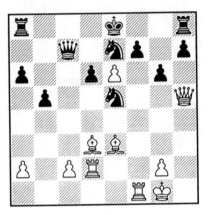

White to move

In this position f7 is the most sensitive square. The Black knight at e5 is so important for Black's defense of this square that White sacrificed his queen for it.

1. Qxe5!	**dxe5**
2. exf7+	

And Black resigned, because of 2. ... Kf8 3. Bh6 mate or 2. ... Kd7 3. Bf5++ Kc6 4. Be4+ Nd5 5. Bxd5 Kd7 6. Bxa8+ and White has a decisive advantage; or 2. ... Kd8 3. Bf5+ Nd5 4. Bg5+ Qe7 5. Rxd5+ and 6. Bxe7 with the same result.

Diagram 117
Spassky – Petrosian, Moscow 1967

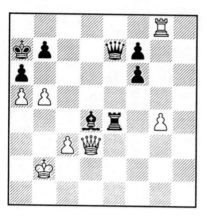

White to move

The Black king is very cramped, and the advance of the b-pawn with check would be decisive, except that the square is defended by the Black bishop. So the point of the combination must be to eliminate the defender, and this can be accomplished by a queen sacrifice.

1. Qxd4+!

And Black resigned in view of 1. ... Rxd4 2. b6 mate.

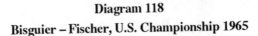

Diagram 118

Bisguier – Fischer, U.S. Championship 1965

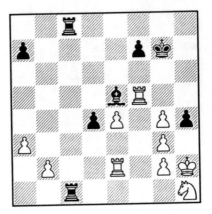

Black to move

The knight at h1 defends the g3 square, which is the focal point of Black's attack. Normally Black would be happy to leave the knight on its worst square in the corner, but here the knight is a critical piece for the defense

1. ...	Rxh1+
2. Kxh1	Rc1+
3. Kh2	Bxg3+

Or 3. ... hxg3+.

| 4. Kh3 | Rh1 mate |

Diagram 119

Instructive example

Black to move

1. ...   Rxg2!

The weak point is f3, and now the threat is 2. ... Nf3+, picking up the queen. So Black, who already has an extra pawn, will win even more material.

Diagram 120

Geller – Novotelnov, Moscow 1951

White to move

1. Rxf8+!

Black resigned, since the end is near:

1. ...	**Kxf8**

1. ... Qxf8 2. Bh7+ Kh8 3. Bg6+ Kg8 4. Qh7 mate.

2. Qh8+	**Kf7**
3. Bg6+!	**Ke6**

Capturing the bishop would allow mate at h5.

4. Qc8+

4. Qg8+ also wins: 4. ... Kd7 5. Bf5+.

4. ...	**Qd7**
5. Bf5+	

And White wins the queen.

Diagram 121
Instructive Example

White to move

In this position after ...

1. Nf7	**Kxf7**
2. Rf1+	**Ke8**

... the only defense here is 2. ... Qxf1 when White should be winning, but more slowly.

3. Rxf8+

White eliminates the defender of the e7-square, and now mate is inevitable.

3. ...	Kxf8
4. Bxe7+	Ke8
5. Bxd6+	Kd8
6. Qe7+	

And 7. Qc7 mate.

Diagram 122
Instructive Example

White to move

1. Nxf6+!

Followed by 2. Qxh7 mate.

Diagram 123

Kupper – Olafsson, Zurich 1959

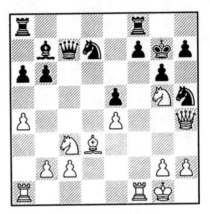

White to move

1. Rxf7+!

And the rook cannot be captured because the e6-square is no longer covered (1. ... Rxf7 2. Ne6+, winning the queen).

Diagram 124

Instructive Example

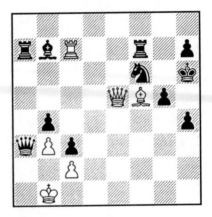

White to move

1. Qxf6+

And White wins (1. ... Rxf6 2. Rxh7 mate or 1. ... Kh5 2. Qxf7+ Kh6 3. Qxh7 mate).

Diagram 125
Instructive Example

White to move

1. Rxg6!   fxg6
2. Rh8!

Winning the queen and finishing up a piece.

Removing the King's Pawn Cover

In this section we'll discuss combinations used to disrupt the pawn chain which defends the castled king. We will see many other thematic examples of exposing the king in Lesson Six.

Diagram 126

Instructive example

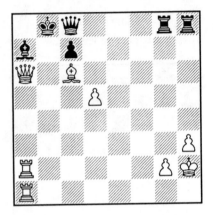

Black to move

White threatens a variety of mates on the queenside, so Black must act quickly. The protective shield of pawns around White's king must somehow be punctured. In this case, the goal is achieved via a rook sacrifice: 1. ... Rxg2+! and now mate follows with 2. ... Qxh3+.

Diagram 127
Instructive Example

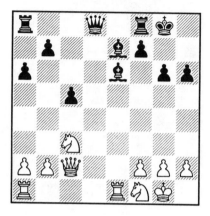

This is a typical example of an exchange sacrifice which fractures the defending pawn structure:

1. Rxe6!	fxg6
2. Qxg6+	Kh8
3. Qxh6+	Kg8
4. Qg6+	

White has already reestablished material equality and now could win a third pawn for an exchange. But White correctly goes for the kill.

4. ...	Kh8
5. Rd1	

Bringing up the reserves!

5. ...	Qe8
6. Qh6+	Kg8
7. Rd3	Rf5
8. Rg3+	Rg5
9. Rxg5	Bxg5
10. Qxg5+	

And White has a material advantage which is sufficient to win.

Diagram 128
Paulsen – Morphy, 1857

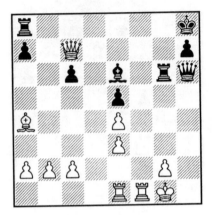

Black to move

This was a blindfold game, but that didn't keep Morphy from seeing

1. ...	Rxg2+!

This eliminates the sole pawn which protects the king from threats on the g-file.

2. Kxg2	Qh3+!
3. Kf2	Qh2+
4. Kf3	Rf8+

And White resigned because of mate on the next move:

5. Qf7	Rxf7 mate

Diagram 129
Instructive example

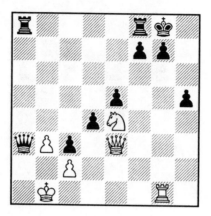

White to move

Black threatens mate at a1 and b2, so White must hurry!

1. Rxg7+	**Kxg7**

Black is forced to take the rook (1. ... Kh8 2. Qh6 mate).

2. Qg5+	**Kh8**
3. Qh6+	**Kg8**
4. Nf6 mate	

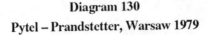

Diagram 130

Pytel – Prandstetter, Warsaw 1979

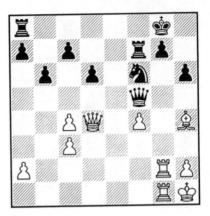

White to move

There are weaknesses in Black's position at g7, f6 and d5. White was able to exploit these weaknesses with precise play:

| **1. Bxf6** | **Qxf6** |
| **2. Rxg7+!** | |

Black resigned here, because the queen will be lost after:

| **2. ...** | **Qxg7** |

Also losing is 2. ... Kh8 3. Rxf7, or 2. ... Kf8 3. Rg8+ Ke7 4. Qxf6+ Kxf6 5. Rxa8.

| **3. Rxg7** | **Rxg7** |
| **4. Qd5+** | |

Diagram 131
Instructive Example

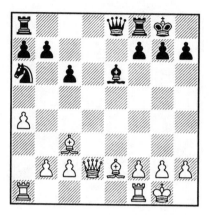

White to move

1. Bxg7	Kxg7
2. Qg5+	Kh8
3. Qf6+!	Kg8
4. Ra3	

And Black is defenseless. The important point is that White was able to bring the rook into the attack.

Diagram 132

Verlinsky – Ryumin, Moscow 1931

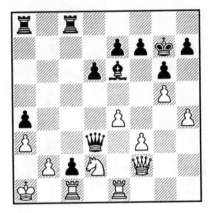

Black to move

1. ...	Rc3!
2. b3	Rxb3

And Black resigned.

Diagram 133

Berry – Seglins, USA 1968

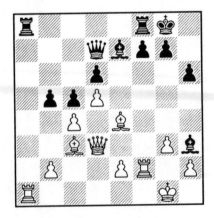

White to move

1. Bh7+	Kh8
2. Rxa8	Rxa8
3. Bxg7+	Kxg7
4. Rxf7+!	Kxf7
5. Qg6+	Kf8
6. Qg8 mate	

All this was forced, and there was no way for Black to escape.

Diagram 134

Arnold – Tchigorin, St. Petersburg 1885

Black to move

The conclusion was rather like a composed study, using the minor pieces to deliver mate.

1. ...	Qxg2+!!
2. Kxg2	Bf3+
3. Kf1	

If the king moves to g3, then the bishop delivers mate at f2.

3. ...	Nh2 mate!

Diagram 135

Kamsky – Lautier, Dortmund 1993

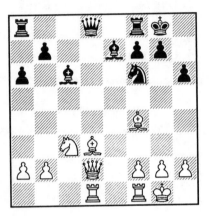

White to move

At the moment, White does not seem to have much of an attack. The attacking pieces are far away, and the Black king seems to be adequately defended by the wall of pawns. Things change quickly!

1. Bxh6!   gxh6
2. Qxh6

By giving away a bishop for two pawns White has managed to destroy the pawn cover of the enemy king and create serious threats to Black's king. Two pawns are not full compensation for a piece, but together with attacking chances they can be enough or more, especially if White can bring in other forces.

By exposing the Black king, White creates new motifs for threats and combinations. White's main problem now is how to get a decisive concentration of force against the enemy king.

2. ...   Re8

This invites White to win the Black queen by playing Bh7+ with a discovered attack on the d-file, but that would not be good for White, who has already sacrificed a bishop. After all, rook and bishop are almost equal to the queen, and rook and two bishops will be stronger here than a queen and two pawns.

3. Bc4!

Black's last move does make some breathing space for the king, but it also has the drawback of weakening the f7-square. White's brilliant move not only takes control of the a2-g8 diagonal but also allows the White queen to make use of the g6-square since the pawn at f7 is now pinned. In addition, the line between the rook at d1 and queen at d8 is now open, and the rook can also transfer to the kingside via d4.

3. ...   Bd7

Black tries to control some light squares, but this doesn't help.

4. Rd4	Bf8
5. Qg6+	Bg7
6. Qxf7+	Kh8
7. Rh4+	Nh7
8. Rxh7+!	Kxh7
9. Qh5+	Bh6
10. Bd3+	Kg8
11. Qxh6	**Black resigns**

Diagram 136

Botvinnik – Keres, The Hague 1948

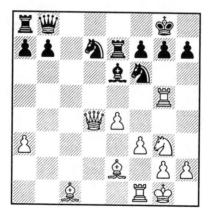

White to move

This happened in the second leg of the World Championship tournament. Black had just played his knight to d7.

1. Rxg7+	Kxg7
2. Nh5+	Kg6
3. Qe3!	

Black resigned, since mate was inevitable.

Diagram 137

Averbakh – N.N., USSR 1955

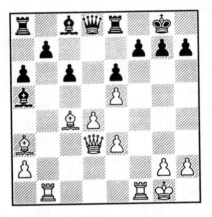

White to move

1. Rxf7!	b5

If Black captures the rook, then after 2. Qxh7 there is the terrible threat of Rf1+.

2. Rbf1!	bxc4
3. Rxg7+!	Kxg7
4. Rf7+!	

White's third rook sacrifice.

4. ...	Kxf7
5. Qxh7 mate	

Diagram 138
Keres – Mikenas, USSR 1946

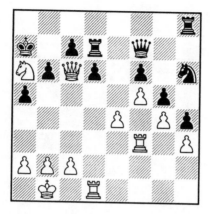

White to move

1. Nc5!

Forcing Black to destroy his own pawn structure.

1. ...   **bxc5**

If Black captures with the d-pawn, then White responds with
2. Rxd7.

2. Ra3!   **Kb8**
3. Rxa5

And mate follows.

Exercises

1

139

White to move

2

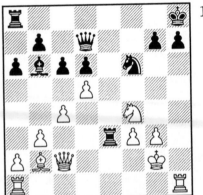

140

White to move

3

141

White to move

4

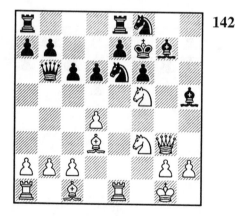

142

White to move

5

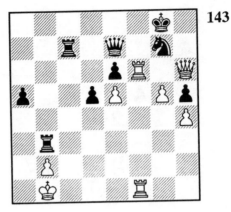

143

Black to move
Find the mate in 6 after 1. ... Rxb2+.

6

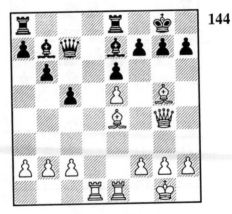

144

White to move

7

White to move

8

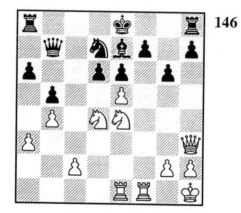

White to move
Continue the combination after 1. Rxf7!.

9

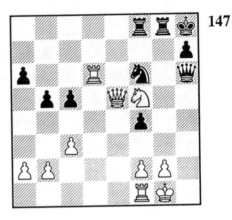

147

Black to move

10

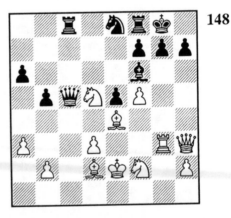

148

White to move

11

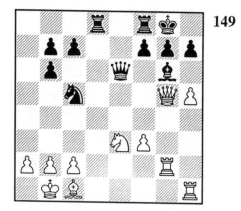

149

Black to move
Can he successfully play 1. ... Qxa2+?

12

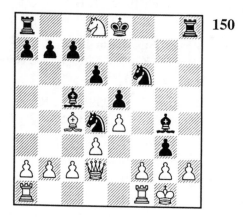

150

Black to move

Solutions

1. Anand-Ivanchuk, Linares 1993: 1. Rxb7+! Kxb7 2. Qa6+ Kb8 3. Qb6+ Ka8 4. Qxc6+ Kb8 5. Qb6+ Ka8 6. Bb5! Black resigns.

2. Flohr-Rovner, Tartu 1950: 1. Rxh7+ Nxh7 2. Rh1. Black resigned because of mate in a few moves, for example 2. ... Kg8 3. Qxh7+ Kf8 4. Ng6+ Kf7 5. Qxg7+ Ke8 6. Rh8 mate.

3. T. Petrosian-Ivkov, USSR vs. Yugoslavia, Belgrade 1979: 1. Rxd4! and Black resigned because the recapture leads to mate in two: 1. ... Rxd4 2. Rxe5+ Kxg4 3. h3 mate.

4. Lechtynsky-Kubichek, Prague 1968: 1. Qxg7+! Nxg7 2. Nh6 mate!

5. Krogius-Lisitsyn, Leningrad 1951: 1. ... Rxb2+! 2. Kxb2 Qb4+ 3. Ka1 Qa3+ 4. Kb1 Rb7+ 5. Kc2 Rb2+ 6. Kc1 Qa1 mate.

6. Batuyev-Abdusamatov, USSR 1951: 1. Bxh7+ Kxh7 2. Bf6! and now: A. 2. ... gxf6 3.Re3! and there is no defense against mate, or B. 2. ... Bf8! 3. Qh5+ Kg8 4. Re3 Qc6 5. Rg3 and Black will lose a lot of material.

7. Fischer-Cooper, Zurich 1959: 1. Bxh6! gxh6 2. Qe3 Bg7 3. f6 Rh8 4. Rf1! Qb5 5. Qf3 Qxb2 6. fxg7 and Black resigned.

8. Boleslavsky-Steiner, Stockholm 1948: 1. ... Qd5 (1. ... Kxf7 2. Qxe6 winning) 2. Rxe7+! Kxe7 3. Qh4+ Kf7 4. Nd6+ Kg7 5. Qe7+ Kh6 6. Re3 and Black resigned.

9. Korsunskaya-Bykova, Riga 1950: 1. ... Rxg2+! 2. Kxg2 Qg5+! and White resigned because of 3. Kh3 Qh5+ 4. Kg2 Rg8+.

10. Steinitz-N.N.: 1. Nxf6+ Nxf6 2. Rxg7+ Kxg7 3. Qh6+ Kg8 4. Qg5+, Black resigns. For example 4. ... Kh8 5. Qxf6+ Kg8 6. Qg5+ Kh8 7. f6 Rg8 8. Qh6 Rg6 9. Bxg6, or 2. ... Kh8 3. Rxh7+! Nxh7 4. f6! and there is no defense against mate.

11. Instructive Example: Black wins with 1. ... Qxa2+! 2. Kxa2 Ra8+ 3. Kb1 Nb3! followed by mate at a1.

12. Knorre-Tchigorin, St. Petersburg 1874: 1. ... Nf3 2. gxf3 Bxf3! and White resigned (3.hxg3 Rh1 mate).

Lesson 6

Destruction of the King's Pawn Cover

In this lesson we will become acquainted with typical combinations where the attacker uses a sacrifice to remove some or all of the pawns protecting the enemy king.

The foundation for such a combination is laid when the attacker has a preponderance of force in the neighborhood of the enemy king. The surplus of attacking force makes it possible for the attacker to invest material in a successful attack. It is important to act decisively when the occasion arises, so that the opponent will not have time to marshal reserve forces and bring them to the defense of the king.

The combinations we will speak of here are well known to experienced chessplayers. We call them *typical combinations* because they occur frequently. Learning them will help you become a strong chessplayer. If the patterns of these combinations becomes familiar, you will not let the opportunity for a winning and striking combination slip through your fingers.

The Sacrifice on f7

All chessplayers know that in the opening the f7-square is the weakest point in Black's camp; therefore, catastrophes are possible on this weak square. However, both in the opening and in the middlegame even experienced masters sometimes

129

overlook the f7 blows. The combinations against f7 in chess practice are quite diverse, but most of them have one thing in common: White's light-squared bishop plays an important role.

In our first example, White has an overwhelming advantage and he brings his White-squared bishop into play.

Diagram 151
Instructive Example

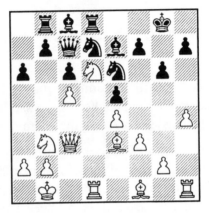

White to move

1. Bc4!	Ndxc5
2. Nxf7!	Kxf7
3. Nxc5	Bxc5
4. Bxc5	Kf6
5. Rxd8	Qxd8
6. f4	

And White has a winning position.

In this example the sacrifice on f7 was the simplest method of exploiting a big positional advantage.

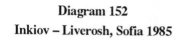

Diagram 152

Inkiov – Liverosh, Sofia 1985

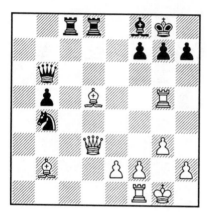

White to move

The following Bxf7 combination draws the Black king from behind its protective cover and leads to the win of material or checkmate.

1. Bxf7+!	**Kxf7**
2. Qxh7	

Threatening to win a third pawn for the piece by Bxg7.

2. ...	**Qh6**
3. Qf5+	**Kg8**
4. Rg6!	**Qd2**

On 4. ... Qh7 White plays 5. Qe6+ and 6. Rh6.

5. Qe6+	**Kh7**
6. Rg4!	**Rc4**

This does not help.

7. e4!

Black resigned.

Diagram 153
Instructive Example

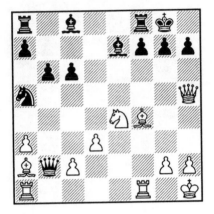

White to move

1. Bxf7+!   Black resigns

On 1. ... Rxf7 2. Qxf7+! Kxf7 3. Be5+ and the discovered check wins, since after the check is repulsed White plays 4. Bxb2 with a decisive advantage. And if Black does not capture the bishop, but plays 1. ... Kh8 instead, then 2. Bg6 h6 3. Bxh6 wins.

Diagram 154
Mecking – Tan, Petropolis 1973

White to move

The Brazilian grandmaster pulled off a stunning coup involving the destructive sacrifice at f7.

1. Bxf7+!

An excellent example of the bishop sacrifice.

1. ...	Kxf7
2. Rxc7+!	

Decoy!

2. ...	Qxc7
3. Qh7+	**Kf6**
4. Qxc7	

White has a decisive advantage and won quickly.

Diagram 155

Tarrasch – Holzhausen, Germany 1906

White to move

White carries out an original combination where first a bishop, and then a knight, are sacrificed.

1. Bxf7+!	Kxf7
2. Ne6!	**Black resigns**

Mate in two follows 2. ... Kxe6? by 3. Qd5+ Kf6 4. Qf5 mate, otherwise White wins the queen.

Sacrificing a Bishop at h7

In the ancient Polerio manuscript we find the following position:

Diagram 156

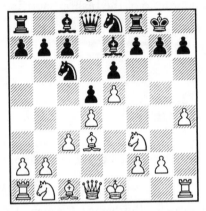

White to move

After 1. Bxh7+ Kxh7 2. Ng5+ Kg8 3. Qh5 Bxg5 4. hxg5 f5
5. g6 or 2. ... Bxg5 3. hxg5+ Kg6 4. Qh5+ Kf5 5. g6+ Black is
mated; and after 2. ... Kg6 3. h5+ Kh6 4. Nxf7 wins the queen.

The main participants here are the bishop, which attacks h7
from its post at d3, the queen on d1 which uses the diagonal to
transfer to the h-file, and the knight on f3 which leaps to g5 with
check. One of the most important parts of the combination is the
White pawn at e5. Since the Black bishop at e7 guards the
g5-square, the combination only succeeds because of the pawn
at h4 backed up by the rook at h1.

Let's consider another example.

Romanovsky-Belov, USSR 1929

**1. e4 Nf6 2. Nc3 d5 3. e5 Nfd7 4. d4 c5 5. dxc5 e6 6. Nf3
Bxc5 7. Bd3 Nc6 8. Bf4 Qb6?**

An error, since Black's development is not sufficient to allow
such excursions.

9. 0-0 Qxb2 10. Nb5! 0-0 11. Rb1 Qxa2

Diagram 157

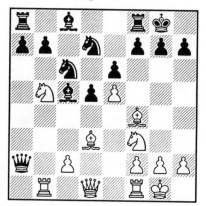

Now a typical combination follows:

12. Bxh7+	**Kxh7**
13. Ng5+	**Kg6**

13. ... Kg8 leads to a quick mate.

14. Qd3+	**f5**
15. Qg3	

Preparing the discovered check.

15. ...	**Rg8**
16. Ne4+	**Kf7**
17. Ned6+	**Bxd6**
18. Nxd6+	**Ke7**
19. Qg5+	

Diagram 158

After 19. ... Nf6 White plays 20. exf6+, and 19. ... Kf8 loses to 20. Qg6. Black resigned.

It often happens that the h7-square lacks sufficient protection when there is no Black knight on f6 — for example, after it has been exchanged:

Diagram 159

Negra – Kreculescu, Bucharest 1957

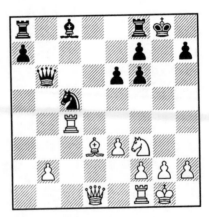

White to move

Now that the knight on f6 has been exchanged, White unleashes the thematic combination:

1. Bxh7+!!	**Kxh7**
2. Ne5!	**Black resigns**

There is a little twist here. The knight headed to e5, instead of g5. But the main idea is the same — the clearing of paths for the heavy artillery.

Diagram 160

Lilienthal – Najdorf, Stockholm 1952

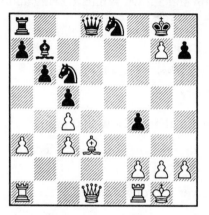

White to move

Even brief analysis of this position shows us why the Bxh7+ sacrifice is likely to succeed:

1. The unfortunate placement of the Black forces, where they cannot come to the king's defense.

2. The possibility to bring White's rooks quickly into the attack.

3. The Black king cannot find shelter on the opposite side of the board.

4. White's pieces are better coordinated. It is true that Black already has two minor pieces for the rook, but this is hardly an asset when the pieces are so poorly stationed.

Such evaluations are important when investigating the secrets of tactical play that are hidden in such positions. Keep in mind that the value of pieces is a relative matter, and that at any given moment an active rook may be superior to two passive minor pieces. Sometimes, it is even stronger than three minor pieces!

1. Bxh7+!

This sacrifice destroys the remaining elements of the Black king's protection and allows White to bring additional forces to deliver the terminal blow.

1. ...   Kxh7

Now Black has three pieces for the rook.

2. Qh5+

The queen enters the attack with tempo!

2. ...   Kxg7
3. Rad1

Still more power is brought to bear!

3. ...   Qf6

Diagram 161

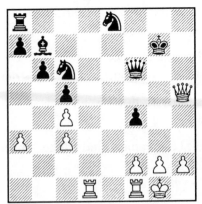

Now Black loses a piece, but even without this the position is hopeless. Note that 3. ... Qc7 loses to 4. Qg4+ and Rd7. If 3.

... Qc8, 4. Rfe1! is decisive after 4. ... Nf6 5. Qg5+ Kf7 6. Rd6 and White wins.

4. Rd7+	**Kf8**
5. Rxb7	**Nd8**
6. Rd7	**Nf7**

Black is trying to regroup, but White does not allow it.

7. Qd5	**Rb8**

7. ... Rd8? loses to 8. Rxf7+.

8. Re1	**f3**
9. Re3	**Black resigns**

Diagram 162

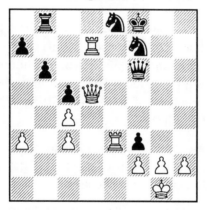

In these two examples we saw the sacrifice of the bishop backed up by concrete variations. But there is another way of looking at things.

Consider the following imaginary position:

Diagram 163
Imaginary position

When Black's knight is on d7, d5 or e8, and the f6-square is not under attack by White's pieces, then 1. Bxh7+ Kxh7 2. Ng5+ Kg8 3. Qh5 may be met by 3. ... Nf6, defending the h7-square and attacking White's queen. The position of the Black rook is also very important — if it is on e8, then White has threats against both f7 and h7.

Black has another defensive plan that must be taken into account. If the Black bishop or queen can get on to the b1-h7 diagonal, White's attack may be repulsed.

Our next position is a good example of defending h7 from the diagonal:

Diagram 164

Hoenlinger – Kashdan, Gyor 1930

White to move

1. Qe5	Nc3
2. Rxc3	

The immediate sacrifice 2. Bxh7+ Kxh7 3. Qh5+ Kg8 4. Ng5 can be beaten back by 4. ... Be4 5. Rxc3 Bg6.

2. ...	bxc3
3. Bxh7+	

White has little choice, though this time the sacrifice does not work.

3. ...	Kxh7
4. Qh5+	Kg8
5. Ng5	Be4!
6. Nxe4	c2
7. Rc1	Rfd8

But not 7. ... Qa3 8. Nf6+ gxf6 9. Qg4+ and White will be able to salvage a draw.

8. h3	f5
9. Ng5	Qxg5!
10. Qxg5	Rd1+
11. Kh2	Rxc1

And White resigned.

Consider this example from a simultaneous exhibition given by a world champion:

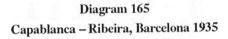

Diagram 165

Capablanca – Ribeira, Barcelona 1935

White to move

This is the position after Black's 13th move. The game continued:

14. Bxh7+!	Kxh7
15. Ng5+	Kg8

On 15. ... Kg6 White would play 16. Qh5+ Kf6 17. N5e4 mate.

16. Rxd7!

And White has destroyed the potential defender of the h7 square.

16. ...   Qxd7

If 16. ... Bxd7, White would play 17. Qh5 Rfe8 18. Qxf7+ Kh8 19. Re1 and Black has no defense, as White threatens to transfer his rook to the h-file.

17. Qh5	**Rd8**
18. Qxf7+	**Kh8**
19. h4	

Immediately 19. Nh5 loses to 19. ... Qd1+.

19. ...	**Qe8**

Diagram 166

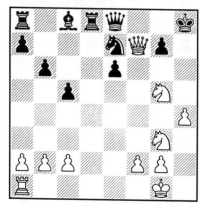

20. Nh5!	**Qf8?**

This allows White an immediate win.

21. Nf6!

The queen cannot be captured because the knight will then deliver the checkmate!

21. ...	**Ng8**
22. Qh5+	

And Black resigned because of 22. ... Nh6 23. Qg6.

Lasker's Combination

In 1889 in a small tournament in Amsterdam, Emanuel Lasker played the following game which made headlines in chess publications all over the world:

Lasker – Bauer, Amsterdam 1889

1. f4 d5 2. e3 Nf6 3. b3 e6 4. Bb2 Be7 5. Bd3 b6 6. Nf3 Bb7 7. Nc3 Nbd7 8. 0-0 0-0 9. Ne2 c5 10. Ng3 Qc7 11. Ne5 Nxe5 12. Bxe5 Qc6 13. Qe2 a6 14. Nh5!

Diagram 167

14. ... Nxh5 15. Bxh7+! Kxh7 16. Qh5+ Kg8

Diagram 168

17. Bxg7!!

The threat is 18. Qh8 mate. If 17. ... f5 then 18. Be5. No better is 17. ... f6 because of 18. Bh6!.

17. ...	Kxg7
18. Qg4+	Kh7
19. Rf3	e5
20. Rh3	Qh6
21. Rxh6	Kxh6
22. Qd7!	

And Black resigned, because White achieves a decisive material advantage.

Let's go back to the position after Black's 14th move.

What is going on here?

1. White's two bishops sit on the long diagonals a1-h8 and b1-h7.

2. Black's king has inadequate protection.

3. White's queen and a rook are in position to support the attack.

Lasker's game produced a great impression on his contemporaries, but nowadays this sort of sacrifice has become rather routine.

Consider the following game:

Nimzowitsch – Tarrasch, St. Petersburg 1914

1. d4 d5 2. Nf3 c5 3. c4 e6 4. e3 Nf6 5. Bd3 Nc6 6. 0-0 Bd6 7. b3 0-0 8. Bb2 b6 9. Nbd2 Bb7 10. Rc1 Qe7 11. cxd5 exd5 12. Nh4 g6 13.Nhf3 (White has lost two tempi with his last two moves.) **13. ... Rad8 14. dxc5** (Creating dynamic chances for Black.) **14. ... bxc5 15. Bb5** (Removing a defender from the kingside.) **15. ... Ne4 16. Bxc6 Bxc6 17. Qc2 Nxd2 18. Nxd2 d4! 19. exd4**

We present this game from the first move to show the mistakes which make this sacrifice possible.

Diagram 169

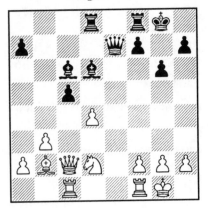

Black to move

Both of Black's bishops are pointed at White's defenseless kingside. Now the stage is set for Lasker's big combination. This time it is Black who earns the honors.

19. ...	Bxh2+
20. Kxh2	Qh4+
21. Kg1	Bxg2
22. f3	

If 22. Kxg2 Black plays 22. ... Qg4+ 23. Kh1 Rd5 24. Qxc5 Rh5+! 25. Qxh5 Qxh5+ 26. Kg2 Qg5+ and 27. ... Qxd2.

22. ...	Rfe8
23. Ne4	

White's valiant defense is not enough to prevent his demise.

23. ...	Qh1+
24. Kf2	Bxf1
25. d5	f5
26. Qc3	Qg2+
27. Ke3	...

Diagram 170

Black to move

Black still needs to play energetically, since White threatens Qg7 mate. Each move must be a check.

27. ...	Rxe4+
28. fxe4	f4+
29. Kxf4	Rf8+
30. Ke5	Qh2+
31. Ke6	Re8+
32. Kd7	Bb5 mate

Of course such combinations do not always succeed. You have to take into account all of the particular features of the position before making the sacrifice, paying special attention to your opponent's defensive resources.

Kirillov – Furman, USSR 1949

1. e4 e5 2. Nf3 Nc6 3. Bb5 a6 4. Ba4 Nf6 5. Qe2 b5 6. Bb3 Be7 7. a4 b4 8. Bd5 Nxd5 9. exd5 Nd4 10. Nxd4 exd4 11. 0-0 0-0 12. Qc4 c5 13. dxc6 dxc6 14. Qxc6 Ra7 15. Qf3 Rc7 16. d3 Bb7! 17. Qd1 Bd6 18. Nd2 Re8 19. Nc4

We provide you with the opening moves of this game to show how combinations are prepared by the previous play. Black does not allow his pawn-grabbing opponent a single moment of respite, which he might use to shore up the defense of the kingside.

Diagram 171

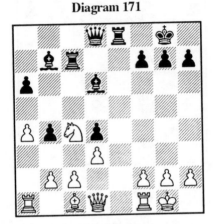

Black to move

Should Black go for the kill here? Before deciding, Furman had to take into account all of the defensive resources available to his opponent.

19. ...	Bxh2+!
20. Kxh2	Qh4+
21. Kg1	Bxg2
22. Kxg2	Rc6
23. Bf4	

23.Qf3! would have put up a more stubborn resistance.

23. ...	Qxf4
24. Rh1	Rf6!

This is a very strong move. 25. f3 will not help because of 25. ... Rg6 26. Kf1 Qg3, and 25. Qd2 will also meet with a tragic fate after 25. ... Rg6+ 26. Kf1 Qg4.

25. Rh2	Rg6+!

And White resigned, because of 26. Kh1 Re1+ 27. Qxe1 Qf3+ 28. Rg2 Qxg2 mate.

The Sacrifice on g7

Diagram 172
Instructive Example

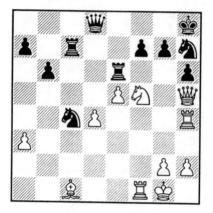

White to move

All of White forces are concentrated for the attack of the enemy king. Black also pulls up his reserves to the main theatre of operations. Black's weakest point is g7 because it is protected only by the King. It is here that White inflicts his first blow opening up the g- and h-files.

1. Nxg7	**Kxg7**
2. Bxh6+!	**Kg8**

2. ... Kh8 3. Bg7+! Kxg7 4. Qxh7+ Kf8 5. Qh8+ Ke7 6. Rxf7+ and Qxd8.

3. Rg4+	**Rg6**
4. e6!	**Nd6**
5. exf7+	**Rxf7**
6. Rxg6+	**Kh8**
7. Rxf7	**Nxf7**
8. Bg7+	
and White wins	

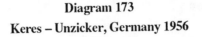

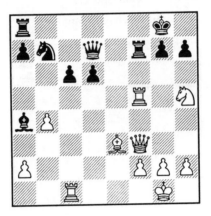

White to move

Black's passive pieces cannot defend his king.

1. Nxg7!   Rxg7

If 1. ... Kxg7 then 2. Bh6+! and now 2. ... Kxh6 3. Rxf7; or 2. ... Kg8 3. Rg5+ Kh8 4. Qc3+; or 2. ... Kg6 3. Qg4+ Kxh6 4. Rh5 mate.

2. Bh6!   Qe7

2. ... Rg6? 3. Rf8+ and 4. Qxf8 mate.

3. Bxg7   Qxg7

Or 3. ... Kxg7 4. h4! with an attack as in the game; *e.g.* 4. ... Rf8 White can play 5. Qg4+ Kh8 (5. ... Kh6 6. Rh5 mate) 6. Qd4+ Kg8 (6. ... Qg7? 7. Rxf8 mate) 7. Rg5+ Kf7 8. Rg7+ wins a queen.

4. h4!

This advance threatens Rg5 and creates an escape square for the king.

4. ...   h6
5. Rc4!

Bringing the other rook into the attack, so Black resigned.

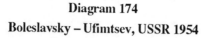

Diagram 174

Boleslavsky – Ufimtsev, USSR 1954

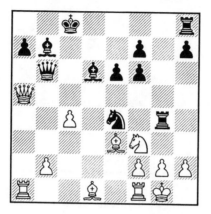

Black to move

1. ...	Rhg8!
2. Ne1	

If 2. Bxb6 then 2. ... Rxg2+ 3. Kh1 Rxh2+! 4. Nxh2 Nxf2 mate, while 2. g3 is met by 2. ... Nxg3 3. hxg3 Rxg3+ 4. fxg3 Qxe3+ 5. Kh1 Qh6+.

2. ...	Rxg2+!
3. Nxg2	Nd2!
4. Qd5	

4. Bxb6 loses to 4. ... Rxg2+ 5. Kh1 Rxh2++ 6. Kg1 Rh1 mate.

4. ...	Bxd5
5. cxd5	Qxb2
6. Bxd2	Qxa1
7. Bf3	Bxh2+

And White resigned.

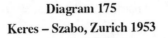

Diagram 175
Keres – Szabo, Zurich 1953

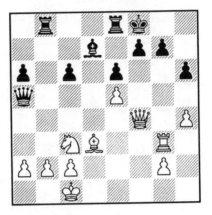

White to move

White must play energetically, otherwise Black will seize the initiative with 1. ... Qb4.

| **1. Rxg7** | **Kxg7** |
| **2. Qf6+** | **Kf8** |

If 2. ... Kg8 then 3. Qxh6 intending 4. Bh7+ Kh8 5. Bg6+ Kg8 6. Qh7+ Kf8 and Qxf7 mate.

3. Bg6!

And Black resigned because of 3. ... Re7 4. Qh8 mate.

Diagram 176
Stein – Portisch, Stockholm 1962

Black's last move was ... Nd7-b6. For a moment, Black has lost control of f6, and Stein takes advantage of it.

1. Nxg7!	**Bxc4**
2. Bf6!	**Be7**

If 2. ... Bxe2 3. Nf5+ Kg8 4. Nh6 mate.

3. Qf3!

And White won. The threat is Ne8+ and if 3. ... Bxf6 then 4. Qxf6 Nd7 5. Rxd7 Qxd7 6. Nh5+ Kg8 7. Qg7 mate.

Diagram 177
Tal – Keres, USSR 1959

Here the sacrifice is dubious.

1. Nxg7?!

White should have played 1. Nxe7+ Rxe7 2. Ne5, but he wants more. Black finds a cold-blooded method of repelling White's attack.

1. ...	Kxg7
2. Ne5	Rh8!
3. Qh3	

A cunning move, threatening 4. Nxf7!.

3. ...	Rh7!

Black needs this rook for defense along the 7th rank.

4. c4	Nf8!
5. Rad1	Rd8
6. Bd2	Qb6
7. Bc3	Kg8!
8. Re3	Ne8!
9. Rg3	Ng7
10. Rdd3	f6
11. Ng6	Nxg6

As the forces are reduced, the attack is also weakened.

12. Rxg6	**Kf7**
13. h5	**Qa6**

And Black is winning.

Exercises

1

178

White to move

2

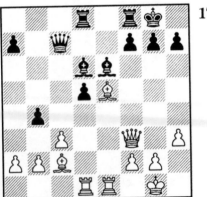

179

White to move

3

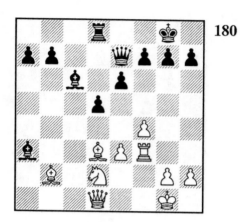

180

White to move

4

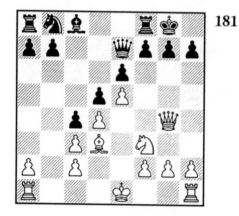

181

White to move

5

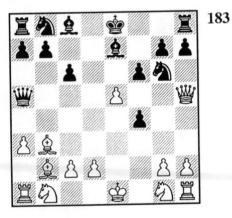

182

White to move

6

183

White to move

7

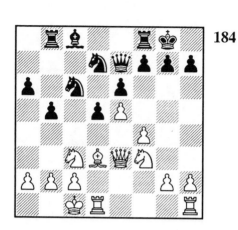

White to move
Is a bishop sac at h7 worthwhile?

8

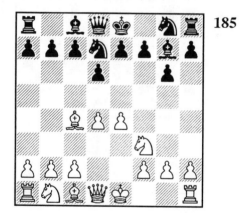

Should White play 1. Bxf7+?

9

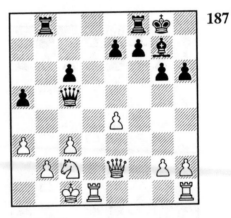

186

White to move

10

187

Black to move

11

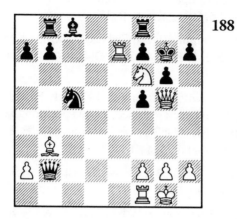

188

White to move

12

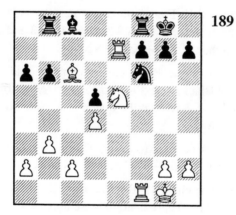

189

White to move

Solutions

1. Instructive example: 1. Nc6! Bxc6 2. Bxh7+! Kxh7 3. Qh5+ Kg8 4. Bxg7! Kxg7 5. Rg3+ Kf6 6. Re1!.

2. Instructive example: 1. Bxh7+! Kxh7 2. Qh5+ Kg8 3. Bxg7! Kxg7 4. Qg5+ Kh7 5. Rd4 Bh2+ 6. Kh1 Qf4 7. Rxf4 Bxf4 8. Qxf4 Rg8 9. Re5.

3. Alekhine-Drewitt, Portsmouth 1923: 1. Bxh7+ Kxh7 2. Rh3+ Kg8 3. Bxg7! and Black resigned. In this position the best move is 3. ... f6 but then 4. Bh6! Qh7 5. Qh5! Bf8 (or 5. ... Be8 6. Rg3+ Kh8 7. Bg7+ and 8. Bxf6+) 6. Qg4+ Kh8 7. Bxf8.

4. Euwe-Marin, 1930: 1. Bxh7+! and Black resigned because of 1. ... Kxh7 2. Qh5+ Kg8 3. Ng5.

5. Instructive Example: 1. Bxh7+ Kxh7 2. Ng5+ Kg8 3. Qh5 Bxg5 4. hxg5 Kf8 5. Qh8+ Ke7 6. Ng6+ fxg6 7. Qxg7 mate.

6. Katalymov-Ilivitsky, USSR 1959: 1. Bf7+ and Black resigned. If 1. ... Kxf7, then 2. e6+ and the queen falls, or 1. ... Kf8 2. Bxg6 and Black is down a lot of material.

7. A variation of the French defense: Yes, the sac works: 1. Bxh7+ Kxh7 2. Ng5+ Kg6 (or 2. ... Kg8 3. Qh3) 3. Qh3 and Black resigned. If 3. ... Ncxe5 then 4. Qh7+ Kf6 5. Nce4+!

8. A variation of the Pirc defense contains this frequently seen predicament of Black: 1. Bxf7+ Kxf7 2. Ng5+ wins for White because 2. ... Ke8 and 2. ... Kf8 lose the queen to 3. Ne6, and 2. ... Kf6 runs into 3. Qf3 mate.

9. Vinogradov - Fedin, Moscow 1973: 1. Qxh6+! gxh6 2. Rxh6+ Kg7 3. Rh7+ Kf8 4. Rh8+ Kg7 5. Rg8+ Kh6 6. g5 mate.

10. Kapengut-Vaganian, 1970: 1. ... Rxb2!! 2. Kxb2 Qxc3+ 3. Kc1 Rb8, White resigns. There is no defense against 4. ... Rb1+ and 5. ... Qb2 mate.

11. Medina-Donner, Beverwijk 1965: 1. Rxf7+, Black resigns (1. ... Rxf7 2. Nh5+ Kg8 3. Qd8 mate).

12. Bronstein-Lehmann, Munich 1958: White's advantage (active pieces) leads to a combination: 1. Nxf7! Bg4 (on 1. ... Rxf7 White had prepared 2. Bxd5! Nxd5 3. Re8+ and 4. Rxf8 mate) 2. Rxf6!, Black resigns (if 2. ... gxf6 3. Nh6+ and 4. Nxg4).

Lesson 7

Combinations with Typical Motifs

Among the various tactical motifs that are encountered during chess battles, there are a few that stand out as the most common. These include *invasion on the back rank, invasion on the seventh rank, overloading*, and *far advanced pawns*. We call these *typical motifs*. In this chapter we will examine combinations which exploit these motifs. We have already seen the concept of undefended pieces at work in Lesson 4, and we will discuss drawing combinations in Lesson 8.

The Back Rank

If there are major pieces (queens and rooks) on the board, then the position of the king on the back row behind a group of unmoved pawns can be quite dangerous, since if the queen or rook infiltrates the back rank, checkmate is possible.

The idea of deflection is often used to exploit a weak back rank. Consider the next position.

Diagram 190
Minic – Honfi, Vrnjacka Banja 1966

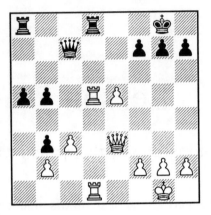

White to move

1.Qa7!!   **Black resigns**

Any capture of the queen reduces the protection of d8, the critical square. But if 1. ... Qc8, then 2. Qxa8 Qxa8 3. Rxd8+ and mates.

Diagram 191
Lemachko – Popova, Moscow 1970

White to move

1.Qxf7+!   **Black resigns**

If 1. ... Rxf7, then 2. Rd8+ Rf8 3. Rxf8 mate.

With queens and rooks on the board there are often mating threats on the back rank. Let's look at a few practical examples.

Diagram 192
Alekhine – Colle, Paris 1925

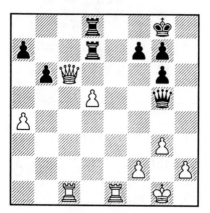

White to move

Black thinks that there is no danger, because a flight square is available at h7. But the back rank still leads to victory for White.

1. Qxd7!	Rxd7
2. Re8+	Kh7
3. Rcc8	

The queen at g5 blocks any further escape by the king.

3. ...	Rd8
4. Rexd8	

And Black resigned.

Diagram 193
Pillsbury – Maroczy, Paris 1900

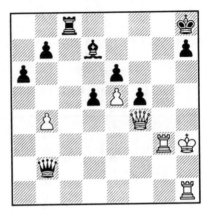

White to move

1. Qh6	Qxe5
2. Qxh7+!	Kxh7
3. Kg2 mate	

Linear mate.

Diagram 194
Vester – Krejcik, Vienna 1937

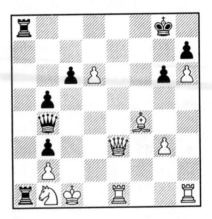

Black to move

Black sacrifices both rooks so that the queen can infiltrate the back rank.

1. ...	Rxb1+
2. Kxb1	Ra1+!
3. Kxa1	Qa5+
4. Kb1	Qa2+
5. Kc1	Qa1+
6. Kd2	Qxb2
7. Kd3	Qc2+
8. Kd4	Qc4+
9. Ke5	Qd5+
10. Kf6	Qf7+
11. Ke5	Qf5+
12. Kd4	c5+
13. Kc3	Qc2 mate!

This happened in a real game!

The 7th Rank

Sometimes the presence of queens and rooks makes it possible to invade the seventh (or second) rank decisively, as in the following game:

Diagram 195

Alatortsev – Capablanca, Moscow 1935

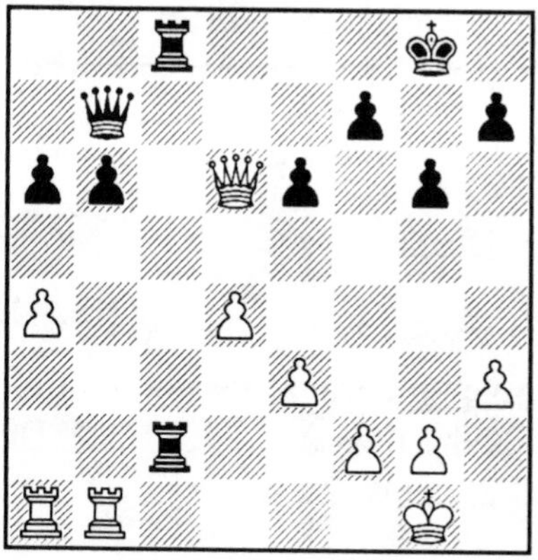

Black to move

In this position Black played ...

1. ...	**Rxf2!**

And after ...

2. Kxf2	**Rc2+**
3. Kg3	

Black wins after 3. Ke1 Qxg2.

3. ...	**Rxg2+**
4. Kh4	**Qe4+**
5. Qf4	**g5+!**

White resigned.

Diagram 196
Instructive Example

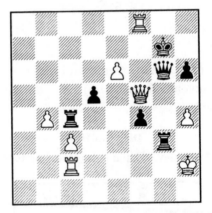

Black to move.

In this position Black plays ...

1. ...	**Rh3+!!**

White has to give up because loss of a lot of material cannot be avoided. If 2. Kxh3 then 2. ... Qg3 mate. But if 2. Qxh3 the in-between move 2. ... Qxc2+ wins.

Overloading

Overloading is what happens to a piece when it has more duties than it can manage.

Diagram 197
Instructive Example

White to move

1. Rb8+	Bxb8
2. Rf8 mate	

The bishop at d6 is overworked. It has responsibilities both at b8 and d8. So by forcing it to surrender control of one of those squares, the other square becomes available.

Diagram 198
Instructive Example

White to move

1. Ra8+	Rc8
2. Rh8+	Re8
3. Rxc8+	Kxc8
4. Rxe8+	

And White has an extra rook. In this case the king became overloaded, with responsibilities to protect both of the rooks.

Diagram 199
Instructive Example

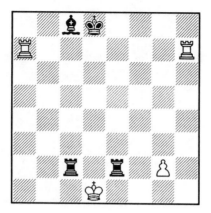

White to move

After 1. Rh8+! the rook at e2 is overloaded. White wins a rook and the game.

Diagram 200
Instructive Example

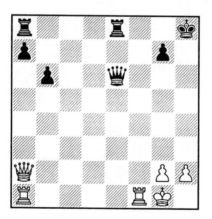

White to move

1. Rf8+ wins after 1. ... Rxf8 2. Qxe6 or 1. ... Kh7 2. Qxe6 Rxe6 3. Rxa8.

Diagram 201
Instructive Example

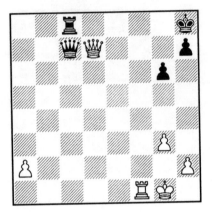

White to move

After 1. Rf8+! the queen is lost because of the overloaded rook at c8.

Diagram 202
Instructive Example

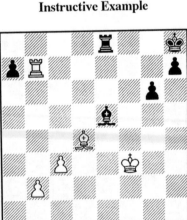

White to move

1. Rb8!

And Black lost a bishop because if 1. ... Rxb8, then 2. Bxe5+.

Here White simultaneously invaded the back row and applied the motifs of *pin* and *fork* with which you are already familiar.

Diagram 203
Instructive Example

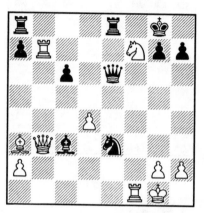

White to move

1. Nh6+	**Kh8!**

Or 1. ... gxh6 2. Rf8+! Rxf8 3. Qxe6+.

2. Rf8+	**Rxf8**
3. Bxf8!	

3. Qxe6? Rf1 mate.

3. ...	**Rxf8**

Not 3. ... Qxb3 because of 4. Bxg7 mate.

4. Nf7!	**Kg8**

Black can't capture on f7 with 4. ... Qxf7 because of 5. Rxf7, or 4. ... Rxf7 because of 5. Rb8+.

5. Qxe6

White has an easy win.

Diagram 204
Instructive Example

White to move

1. Bxf7+!

This is a typical exploitation of an overloaded piece. Black cannot capture at f7 with the king and simultaneously protect the queen at d8.

2. ...	Ke7
3. Bg5+	Kxf7
4. Qxd8	Bb4+
5. Qd2	

White emerges with an extra pawn.

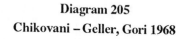

Diagram 205

Chikovani – Geller, Gori 1968

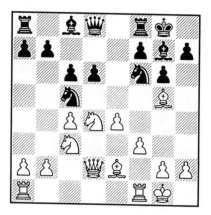

Black to move

Here the queen is overloaded, being responsible for the safety of the knight at d4 and the bishop at g5.

1. ...	Nfxe4
2. Nxe4	Nxe4
3. fxe4	Bxd4+

And here is where the overloading comes in. If 4. Qxd4 then 4. ... Qxg5 5. Qxd6 when White restores material equality but has the worse pawn structure and a positional disadvantage. Black's edge is enough. After all, not all combinations give mate.

Diagram 206
Simagin – Nikolic, 1968

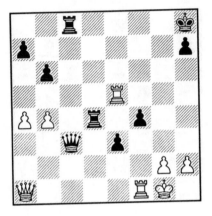

White to move

1. Re8+!   **Kg7**

Black cannot capture at e8 without losing the queen at c3.

2. Rxc8

Black resigned, as his queen was overloaded.

Diagram 207
Botvinnik – Chekhover, Moscow 1935

White to move

White has successfully disrupted the pawn cover of the Black king, and the attack is proceeding well. The Black forces are huddled on the queenside and cannot participate in the defense. The only thing holding his position together is the knight at f6, which covers the critical square h7. Of course, Black has a material advantage of two pieces for three pawns.

White's pieces, on the other hand, are well placed, except for the rook at a1, but even that is only a couple of moves away. So it is natural to eliminate the mighty defender at f6.

1. Rxf6!

Now Black's pieces are overworked. He keeps the extra piece but loses the game.

1. ...	Bxf6

1. ... gxf6? allows mate after 2. Qh7+.

2. Qh7+	Kf8
3. Re1!	

Bringing the rook into the game and decisively cutting off the Black king on the e-file.

3. ...	Be5

Otherwise Qh8 will be checkmate. From here on White checks the Black king relentlessly until it is mated.

4. Qh8+	Ke7
5. Qxg7+	Kd6
6. Qxe5+	Kd7
7. Qf5+	Kc6
8. d5+	Kc5
9. Ba3+	Kxc4
10. Qe4+	Kc3
11. Bb4+	Kb2
12. Qb1 mate	

Far Advanced Pawn

A pawn that has advanced far into enemy territory can be very dangerous, not only in the endgame but even in the opening and middlegame.

Natapov-Razdobarin, Krasnoyarsk 1969

1. f4	e5
2. fxe5	d6
3. exd6	Bxd6
4. Nf3	g5
5. e4?	

The correct moves are 5. g3 and 5. d4.

5. ...	g4
6. Ng1	

If 6. e5, then 6. ... gxf3 7. exd6 Qh4+ 8. g3 Qe4+ 9. Kf2 Qd4+! 10. Ke1 f2+ 11. Ke2 Bg4 mate.

6. ...	Qh4+
7. Ke2	g3
8. Nc3	

Diagram 208

Black to move

8. ...	Qxh2!
9. Rxh2	gxh2
10. Nf3	h1=Q

The pawn has completed its journey to the last rank, and Black has an extra rook. After a few more moves, White resigned.

Here is an example of a successful fight against a deeply advanced pawn.

Palatnik – Mikenas, Vilnius 1975

1. c4 Nf6 2. Nf3 e6 3. g3 d5 4. Bg2 c6 5. b3 a5 6. 0-0 a4 7. cxd5 axb3?

Better is 7. ... exd5 8. bxa4.

8. dxc6   ...

Diagram 209

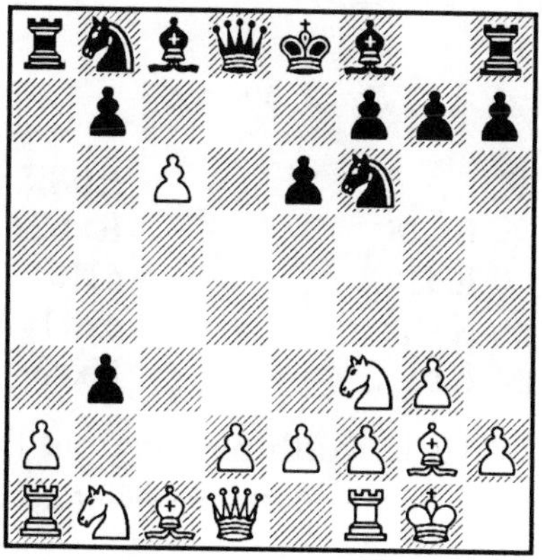

Black to move

8. ... Rxa2 9. c7! Qxc7 10. Rxa2 bxa2 11. Qa4+ Nc6 12. Qxa2 and White stands better.

Opening analysis by GM Efim Geller

1. d4 Nf6 2. c4 g6 3. Nc3 Bg7 4. e4 d6 5. f3 0-0 6. Be3 e5 7. d5 c6 8. Qd2 cxd5 9. cxd5 a6 10. 0-0-0 Nbd7 11. Nge2 b5 12. Kb1 Nb6 13. Nc1 b4 14. Bxb6 bc 15. Qe3

Now follows a beautiful variation.

Diagram 210

Black to move.

15. ...	Rb8!!
16. Bxd8	Rxb2+
17. Ka1	c2!!
18. Kxb2	cxd1=N+!
19. Kb1	Nxe3

And Black wins. It is worth pointing out that as the pawn approaches the promotion square its power grows.

Yu-Ivanchuk, Lucerne 1993

1. d4 d5 2. c4 e6 3. Nf3 dxc4 4. Qa4+ Nd7 5. e4 Nf6 6. Nc3 a6 7. Bxc4 Rb8 8. Qc2 b5 9. Be2 Bb7 10. 0-0?

Diagram 211

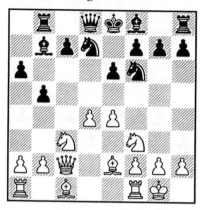

Black to move

10. ...	**b4!**
11. e5	**bxc3**
12. exf6	**cxb2**
13. fxg7	

Better is 13. Bxb2 Nxf6 14. Ne5 with compensation for the pawn.

Diagram 212

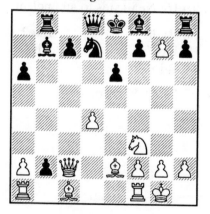

Black to move

13. ...	bxa1=N!
14. gxh8=Q	Nxc2
15. Bg5	

Diagram 213

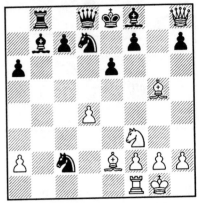

Black to move

15. ...	Bxf3!

Not only do we have a rare combination involving pawns, but as a bonus there is a queen sacrifice!

Instead 15. ... f6 16. Ne5 leads to an unclear position.

16. Bxd8	Bxe2
17. Bxc7	Rb7
18. Bd6	

If 18. Rc1 Rxc7 19. Qxh7 Nf6.

Diagram 214

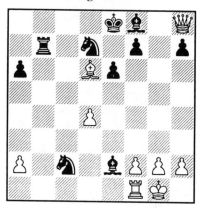

Black to move

18. ...	Bxf1
19. Kxf1	Rb6
20. Bxf8	Nxf8

And Black later converted his material advantage into a win.

Diagram 215

Karpov – Kasparov, Linares 1993

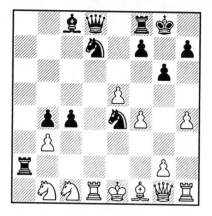

Black to move

1. ...	c3!!

Black sacrifices a rook.

2. Nxa2   c2

A double attack in the form of a pawn fork.

Diagram 216

White to move

3. Qd4

3. Rc1 would have been met by 3. ... Nxe5! 4. Rxc2 Bg4! 5. Nd2 Qd3!! sacrificing the queen, though its capture leads to mate by the knight: 6. Bxd3? Nxd3+ 7. Kf1 Ng3 mate.

Analysis diagram

Position after 7. ... Ng3 mate

But if 6. Nxe4, then 6. ... Qxe4+ 7. Re2 Bxe2 8. Bxe2 Ra8 and Black wins.

After **3. Qd4** the game continued:

3. ...	**cxd1=Q+**
4. Kxd1	**Ndc5!**
5. Qxd8	**Rxd8+**
6. Kc2	**Nf2**

Here Karpov ran out of time, but mate was coming anyway: 7. Rg1 Bf5+ 8. Kb2 Nd1+ 9. Ka1 Nxb3 mate, or 9. Kc1 Nxb3 mate.

Exercises

1

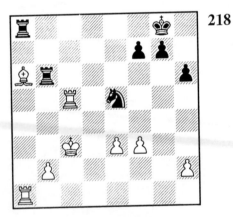

217

White to move

2

218

White to move

3

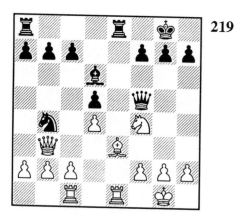

219

Black to move

4

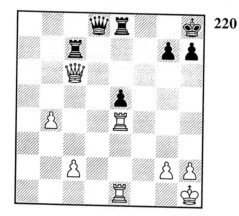

220

White to move

5

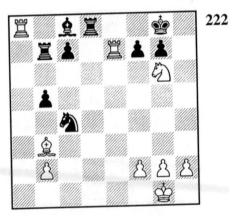

221

White to move

6

222

White to move

7

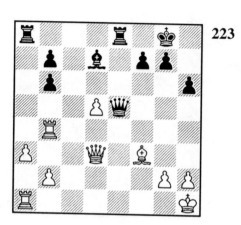

223

Black to move

8

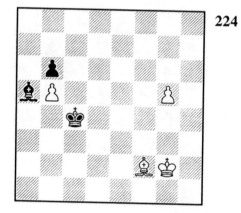

224

White to move

9

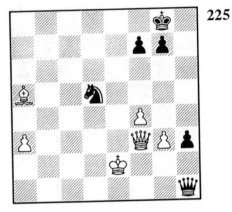

225

Black to move

10

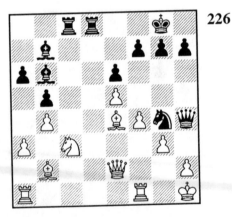

226

Black to move

11

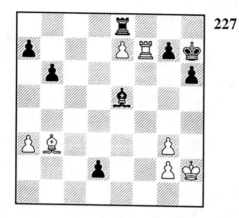

227

White to move

12

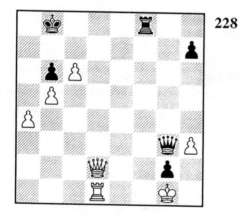

228

Black to move

Solutions

1. Palatnik-Sveshnikov, Leningrad 1976: 1. Rd8+ Kh7 2. Qf5+ g6 3. Qxf7+ Qg7 4. Re7 Qxf7 5. Rxf7 mate.

2. Capablanca-Rossolimo, Paris 1933: 1. Bd3! and Black resigned because of 1. ... Re8 2. Rxe5!.

3. Capablanca-Alekhine, Buenos Aires 1927: 1. ... Nxc2! (a deflection from the back rank) 2. Rxc2 (2. ... Qxc2 3. Rxc2 Rxc2 4. Bxf4) 2. ... Qxf4 and Black has an extra pawn and a better position.

4. Botvinnik-Boleslavsky, Leningrad 1941: White exploited the weakness of the back rank and simplified the position into a winning endgame with 1. Qxe8! Qxe8 2. Rxe5 Qg8 3. Re8 Rxc2 4. Rxg8 Kxg8 5. Rb1 and White won.

5. Aitkin-Paine, England 1962: 1. Qh6 Qxf6 2. Rd8+! and Black resigned because of 2. ... Bxd8 3. Qf8 mate.

6. Tal-N.N., Tbilisi 1965: 1. Rd7!!. This move vacates the square and overloads Black's position: 1. ... Rxd7 2. Rxc8+ Kh7 3. Nf8+ with a fork; or 1. ... Re8 2. Rxc8! Rxc8 3. Ne7+ and again there is a fork.

7. Mikenas-Bronstein, 23rd USSR Championship 1954: 1. ... Rxa3!!. White resigned. A brilliant example of exploiting overloading and a back-rank weakness.

8. Bannik-Nikolayevsky, Odessa 1958: 1. Bxb6!! Bc3 2. Ba5!! and Black resigned, since one of the passed pawns will queen.

9. Medina-Tal, Palma de Mallorca 1966: 1. ... Qxf3+! 2. Kxf3 Ne3!! and the deflection creates an unstoppable passed pawn, so White resigned.

10. Rotlevi-Rubinstein, Russia 1909: 1. ... Rxc3!! 2. gxh4 (2. Bxc3 Bxe4+ overloads the queen — 3.Qxe4 Qxh2 mate) 2. ... Rd2!! (deflection) 3. Qxd2 Bxe4+ 4. Qg2 (pinning) 4. ... Rh3! (exploiting the pin) and White resigned since Rxh2 is coming.

11. Duckstein-Kaluanasaram, Delhi 1961: 1. Bc2+ Kg8 2. Rf8+! Rxf8 3. Bb3+ (The bishop returns to b3 with decisive results after 3. ... Kh8(h7), or after 3. ... Rf7 White will queen his pawn.

12. N.N.-Capablanca, New York 1942: 1. ... Rf1+! 2. Rxf1 Qh2+!! (decoy) 3. Kxh2 gxf1=N+!! with a decisive fork.

Lesson 8

Drawing Combinations

There is a well-known aphorism in the chess community that "it is never too late to resign." The examples in this chapter will serve to illustrate this concept.

When teetering on the precipice, faced with almost certain loss, a chessplayer does not want to come to terms with his fate. He tries to save himself through some sort of combination, leading to stalemate, perpetual check or repetition of the position.

Stalemate

A stalemate often occurs when one of the opponents makes a serious error in a won position.

Diagram 229
Fichtl – Blatny, Bratislava 1956

White to move

In this position White, who enjoyed a decisive material advantage, carelessly played:

1. d6??

This move sets up the stalemating combination.

1. ...   Bc6+!!
2. Qxc6

Capturing the bishop is forced, but now the Black king has nowhere to go, and in order to reach stalemate all that remains is to get rid of the rook.

2. ...   Rg1+
3. Kxg1   Stalemate

Diagram 230
Instructive Example

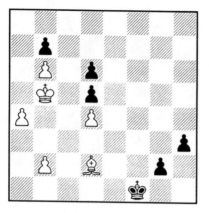

White to move

White has an extra bishop, but it is in no position to stop both of the Black pawns. It is often difficult to eliminate one's own bishop to achieve stalemate, because it is hard to force the opponent to capture it. But here there is another way:

1. Ba5!	**g1=Q**
2. b4!	

And no matter what Black does, White is stalemated.

Diagram 231
Composition by C. Bent (final part)

White to move

In this example White saves the half point using the stalemating idea, even though three pieces must be jettisoned to do so!

1. Ne7+	**Bxe7**

Black must capture or he loses his queen.

2. Nd6+!	**Bxd6**
3. Bg4!	**Qxg4**

Stalemate

Diagram 232

Pitch – Iux, Berlin 1963

Black to move

Although the Black king has some room to maneuver, there is still a stalemate available if only Black can get rid of the knight (getting rid of the queen is rarely difficult).

1. ...	**Qc6+**
2. Kf5	**Ng7+**
3. Bxg7	

Otherwise White loses the queen.

3. ...	**Qg6+!**

And however White captures, it is stalemate.

Diagram 233
Instructive Example

White to move

In the battle of queen vs. rook the stronger side usually wins, though it must watch out for drawing resources based on stalemate.

1. Rh7+	**Kg5**

1. ... Kg6? 2. Rh6+ draws.

2. Rg7+	**Kh6**

Or 2. ... Kf6 3. Rg6+! Kxg6 stalemate while 2. ... Kf5 3. Rf7+ Ke5 4. Re7 also draws.

3. Rh7+!

And the game ends in stalemate or perpetual check.

Perpetual Check

Perpetual check arises when one player can continuously give check to the enemy king. This leads to the game being drawn, and many combinations are built on this idea.

Diagram 234
Instructive Example

White to move

Black enjoys a huge material advantage, but his pieces are misplaced.

1. Qe5+	**Qgg7**
2. Qe8+	**Qhg8**
3. Qh5+	**Q7h7**
4. Qe5+	

And it is clear that the game must end in a draw.

Diagram 235
Instructive Example

White to move

Here, too, White escapes by perpetual check.

1. Rxg7+!   **Kxg7**

If 1. ... Kh8, White plays 2. Rxh7+ which also leads to a draw by perpetual check.

2. Qg5+	**Kh8**
3. Qf6+	**Kg8**
4. Qg5+	

With perpetual check.

Here is yet another variation on this theme:

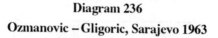

Diagram 236
Ozmanovic – Gligoric, Sarajevo 1963

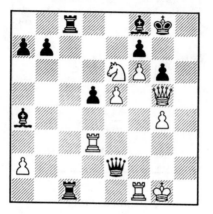

White to move

White's attack is getting nowhere, and Black has an extra piece and a strong counterattack. So White bails out with a perpetual check.

1. Qxg6+!	fxg6
2. f7+	Kh7

2. ... Kh8? loses to 3. Rh3+.

3. Rh3+	Bh6
4. Ng5+	Kg7
5. Ne6+ with perpetual check	

Diagram 237
Walbrodt – Mieses, Berlin 1884

White to move

1. fxg6!	Nc3+
2. Qxc3!	

Obviously not 2. bxc3?? bxc3+ with a discovered check that wins, since after 3. Ka1 Qxa2+ 4. Kxa2 Rb2+!! 5. Ka3 (or 5. Ka1) Black mates with 5. ... Ra8+.

2. ...	bxc3
3. Nf5+	Kg8

Not 3. ... Kh8? 4. g7+ Kg8 5. Nh6 mate.

4. Ne7+

And the position is a draw, since 4. ... Kg7 is met by 5. Nf5+, etc.

Diagram 238

Radevich – Donskikh, USSR 1972

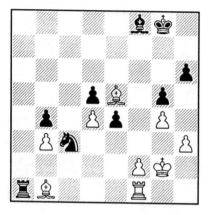

White to move

1. Bxe4!!

1. Bc2 would be a mistake because of 1. ... Ra2! 2. Bb1 Rb2!.

1. ...	Rxf1

2. Bf5!

And a draw was agreed, since 2. ... Ra1 is met by 3. Be6+ Kh7 4. Bf5+ Kg8 5. Be6+.

Pursuit

Pursuit is the term we use for situations where a less valuable piece endlessly chases a more valuable enemy piece. This can lead to cases of perpetual check when the more valuable piece is the king, or a forced draw by repetition when the enemy piece is something other than the king. Obviously it is unlikely that the pursuer will be a pawn, or even a knight, as these pieces have a limited range. But there are some exceptions, when a knight combines with another piece.

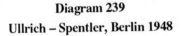

Diagram 239

Ullrich – Spentler, Berlin 1948

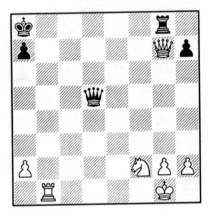

White to move

White, who is a piece up, threatens Qb7 mate if the Black queen leaves the a8-h1 diagonal, but Black threatens … Qxg2 mate if White abandons the g-file.

1. Rb5!

1. Rd1? Qxd1!+ 2. Nxd1 Rxg7, and Black wins.

1. ...		**Re8!!**

Threatening a back rank mate.

2. Rb1!		**Rg8!**
3. Rb5!		**Draw**

Diagram 240

Sax – Mariotti, Las Palmas 1978

Black to move

1. ...	Nxe3!
2. Rxc2	Ra1+!
3. Kh2	Nf1+

And the game is drawn, since the knight will shuttle between e3 (with the rook at a1 providing discovered check) and f1, where it attacks the king directly.

Diagram 241
Yudasin – Kir. Georgiev, Manila 1990

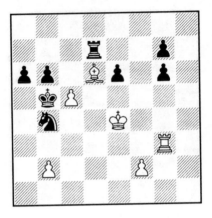

White to move and draw

1. c6!!	Nxc6

Other captures fail: 1. ... Kxc6 2. Bxb4 and 1. ... Rxd6 2. c7 Rc6 3. Rc3!.

2. Rb3+	Ka5
3. Ra3+	Kb5
4. Rb3+	

Drawn by perpetual check.

Exercises

1

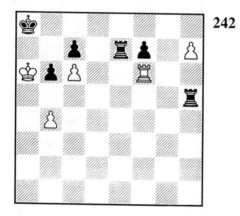

242

White to move

2

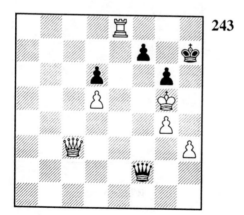

243

Black to move

3

White to move

4

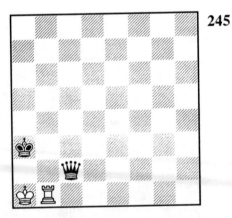

White to move

5

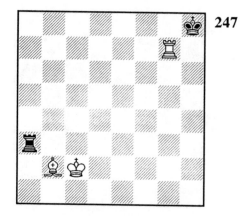

White to move

6

Black to move

7

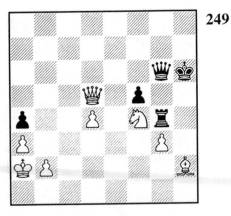

248

Black to move

8

249

Black to move

9

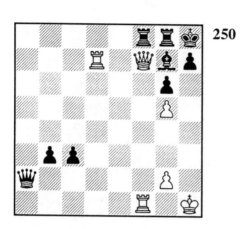

White to move
Find a draw by perpetual check.

10

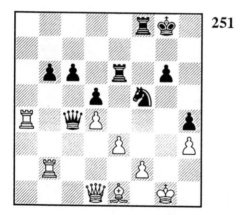

Black to move. His queen is lost! How can you save the position by exploiting the vulnerability of the White king?

11

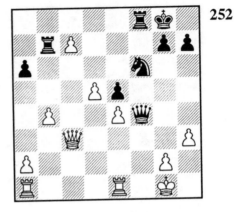

252

Black to move
Perpetual check can save Black.

12

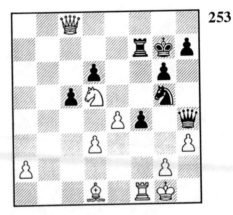

253

Black to move
By sacrificing a knight and a rook,
Black can make a draw in this difficult position.

Solutions

1. Marshall-McClure, New York 1923: 1. Rh6!! Rxh6 2. h8=Q+ Rxh8 3. b5. Black has two extra rooks but can't avoid the stalemate.

2. Najdorf-Cartier, Mar del Plata 1984: 1. ... f6+ 2. Qxf6 Qh4+! 3. Kxh4 (3. Kf4 drops the queen) 3. ... g5+ 4. Kxg5 stalemate.

3. D.Gurgenidze, 1986: 1. Qe3+! Kxe3+ 2. Rg3++ Kf2 stalemate.

4. Instructive Example: 1. Rb3+ Ka4 (either capture at b3 leads to stalemate) 2. Rb4+ Ka5 3. Rb5+ Ka6 4. Rb6+ Ka7 5. Rb7+ Ka8 6. Rb8+ with perpetual check or stalemate.

5. G. Mattison, 1931: 1. Kh1! Qxf2 stalemate.

6. R.Bianchetti, 1925: 1. ... Rc3+! 2. Bxc3 stalemate or 2. Kxc3 Kxg7 or 2. Kb1 Kxg7 with a draw in each case.

7. Krangame-Treger, Augsburg 1938: 1. ... g5+! 2. Kh3 g4+ (pursuit) 3. Kxg4 stalemate.

8. N.N.-Juhly, Zurich 1900: 1. ... Rxf4! 2. gxf4 Qf7!! 3. Qxf7 stalemate.

9. Bootyaroo-Szabo, Rumania 1956: 1. Qxg7+! Rxg7 2. Rxf8+ Rg8 3. Rff7 Rc8 4. Rxh7+ with a draw, since 4. ... Kg8 5. Rhg7+ etc.

10. Kopayev-Vistanetskis, USSR 1949: 1. ... Qf1+!! 2. Kxf1 Nxe3+ 3. Ke2 Nc4+! 4. Kf1 Ne3+!.

11. Unzicker-Averbakh, Stockholm 1952: 1. ... Rxc7! 2. Qxc7 Ng4! 3. hxg4 Qf2+ 4. Kh2 Qh4+ with a draw.

12. Smirin-I. Ivanov, USA 1990: 1. ... Rf5!! 2. Qd7+ Kh6 3. exf5 Nxh3+! with a draw because of 4. gxh3 Qg3+ 5. Kh1 Qxh3+ with perpetual check, or 4. Kh2 Nf2+ 5. Kg1 Nh3+ repeats the position.

Lesson 9

How to Calculate Variations

In this lesson we will learn the art of calculation, one of the most important factors in an actual tournament chess game. We have already discussed the fact that combinations are not available in every position, and despite the numerous examples presented in this book they are, in fact, quite rare. More often victory is achieved through careful planning and accurate calculation, all of which must be accomplished within the limitations imposed by the time control.

Chess calculation is not a simple matter of "If I move here, he'll move there" repeated over and over. Calculating chess variations is a winnowing process of first selecting a set of moves to consider as *candidates,* and then using the time available to examine these candidates in sufficient detail. In this way you chart the course of the game, at least in the short term. You must also consider your opponent's replies to each candidate move based on their apparent merit. This is not a simple matter. We have neither the time nor the mental capacity to examine every possible move deeply and thoroughly. Computers do that. Until quite recently, computers simply calculated all possible replies to all possible moves. Suppose you have a position with 30 legal moves (most positions have even more possibilities). If you look at each position for ten seconds, just to evaluate it by counting material or some other simplistic method, then the first move takes 300 seconds, or five

214

minutes to work out. But of course in reply to each of your 30 moves, the opponent may have 30 different replies, so that zooms to 150 minutes, and you are still at move one. Since most tournaments only allow you two hours for 40 moves by each player, this method simply isn't practical.

It is also inefficient, because some of these candidate moves can be rejected immediately. Your opponent may have a simple reply like grabbing your queen or checkmating in a single move. So the first thing we need to do is narrow the search to only those moves which both advance your own plan and which do not allow the opponent to respond with a winning reply. In this connection we must also take into account psychological factors, various ways of thinking, and other variables we will discuss later. Oversights are possible, and not infrequent, even in the simplest of positions, for reasons which have interested psychologists for several decades.

Learning to Calculate Variations

When calculating variations, there are all sorts of ways to go wrong, and even in grandmaster experience mistakes are often made. It is easy enough to overlook a reply to a single move, and the situation becomes much more complicated as you deepen the search to two, three, four and five moves. In each case you have to find the very best move for yourself and must take into consideration the best possible reply by your opponent.

It is obvious, then, that you need a good training method for calculating variations. Here is our suggested approach for learning to calculate:

1. In a given position, analyze the most tactically complicated lines.

2. Taking into account the amount of time at your disposal, calculate concrete variations. Take 10 to 30 minutes, and write out the variations you have found. Then compare them with the published commentaries, or go over them with your teacher.

3. Use published works that contain lots of diagrams, working without moving the pieces at the board. Try to solve combinations, endgame studies and other test positions.

4. Computers and chess game databases are also very helpful in learning tactical patterns. Many books and chess materials are now available in this format. Database programs are especially helpful because they provide a diagram on every move

There are three very important factors in tactical training. First, look as deeply as necessary into the position, considering all the subtle factors as you extend your search. At first you must try to work out all the lines to a tactical conclusion. Later you will be able to rely on your evaluation of positions to know when you have looked deeply enough.

Second, you must develop a sense of when to "prune" the "tree of variations." That is, you must know which branches of the given variation are worth pursuing. Remember that each move you consider opens up lots of new possibilities, and it is simply impossible for a human being, as opposed to a computer, to look at all of them. You will just waste energy and precious time looking at moves that simply do not matter.

Third, you have to remember the difference between training conditions and actual play, and fine-tune your analytical method to work within the limitations of tournament play and the time control involved. So you ought to limit your examination of any position to 20-30 minutes.

The art of tactical analysis is best acquired by working from examples of the games of great tacticians.

Diagram 254

Capablanca – Marshall, New York 1909

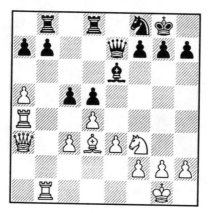

Black to move

Spend 15 minutes on your calculations. When deciding on your aim in this position, notice that White's Ra4 is not well placed.

1. ...	Bd7
2. Bb5	Bf5

Attacking the rook on b1.

3. Rc1	a6

Attacking the bishop.

4. Be2	Bd7

Black wins the exchange.

This is a classic four-move forced maneuver *without* sacrifices. Black played only attacking moves, and on each turn White was forced to retreat.

Diagram 255
Study by Birnov

White to move

Spend five minutes on this position.

In this example Black's knight on b4 not only comes under attack but also blocks his king when it retreats. Here White must think about playing checks with his rook. Black's misplaced a8-knight is an important feature of the position.

1. Kc3	**Na6**

If 2. ... Na2+ 3. Kb3 White wins the knight.

2. Rb1+	**Ka7**

The only move to hold the knight at a8.

3. Rb7 mate

Diagram 256
Palatnik – Klubis, Odessa 1971

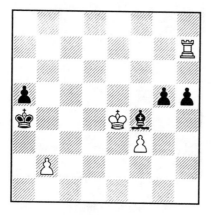

White to move

White is ahead the exchange for a passed pawn. If he plays 1. Rxh5 Black answers 1. ... Kb3 and wins the b2-pawn, with a likely draw. But White can play for a win by exploiting Black's awkward king position.

1. Rb7

Black must now think about his king, and his counterplay is his passed h-pawn.

| 1. ... | h4 |

Now try to calculate what happens next.

| 2. Kd4 | h3 |
| 3. Kc4 | h2 |

Diagram 257

White to move

If you have calculated this far you are doing well. Black's h-pawn is about to queen. If your calculations foresaw only 4. Rh7 here, then your analysis was not fully successful. But if you saw that now 4. Rb3 (threatening 5. Ra3 mate) forces 4. ... Bd6 (in order to answer 5. Ra3+ with 5. ... Bxa3), then that's great!

4. Rb3	**Bd6**
5. Ra3+!	**Bxa3**

Obstruction.

6. b3 mate

Diagram 258
Study by Kasparian

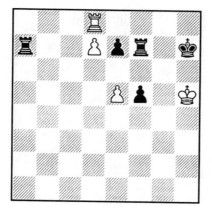

White to move

Study this position for 10 minutes.

How can White win? Neither 1. Rh8+ Kxh8 2. d8=Q+ Kh7, nor 1. e6 Rg7 2. Rc8 Ra1! (threatening ... Rh1 mate) is successful. The solution is simple.

1. Re8!	Rxd7
2. e6	

And White wins with a fork.

Diagram 259

Jacks – Pinch, England 1974

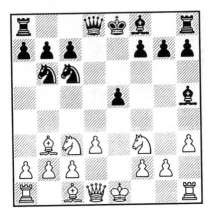

White to move

Analyze this position. The motif of this combination is the possibility to drive the Black king into the center.

1. Nxe5!	**Bxd1**

If 1. ... Nxe5 2. Qxh5 with an extra pawn.

2. Bxf7+	**Ke7**
3. Bg5+	**Kd6**

The only move.

4. Ne4+!

Not 4. Bxd8? Nxe5 with an extra piece for Black.

4. ...	**Kxe5**

Perhaps Black's king can defeat all of White's pieces by himself?

5. f4+	**Kd4**

Or 5. ... Kf5 6. Ng3 mate.

6. Rxd1

If you reached this position from analyzing 1. Nxe5! then you did very well. Seeing this position would be enough for you to make the decision to play 1. Nxe5! because the Black king is now a prisoner in White's camp.

| **6. ...** | **Qxg5** |

If 6. ... Qd7 7. c3+ Ke3 8. f5 mate.

| **7. c3+** | **Ke3** |
| **8. 0-0!** | |

Threatening 9. Rf3+ Ke2 10. Rd2+ Ke1 11. Rf1 mate.

| **8. ...** | **Qc5** |
| **9. Ng3!** | |

Now the threat is 10. Rf3 mate.

| **9. ...** | **Nd4** |

To hold the f3-square.

| **10. Rf2!** | |

Planning 11. Nf1 mate.

| **10. ...** | **Ne2+** |

This diverts the knight from f1, but it does not save the king.

| **11. Nxe2** | **Na4** |
| **12. Kf1** | **Black resigns** |

The threat is 13. Rf3 mate, and if 12. ... Qc6 (to hold f3) 13. Nd4 and Black cannot stop 14. Nc2 mate or 14. Nf5 mate.

An important conclusion to draw from this example is that *a lengthy calculation is easier to make if you use the same motif throughout the entire combination.*

Avoiding Errors in Calculation

When calculating variations many chessplayers, even strong ones, make inaccurate moves and serious mistakes. Many of these are because of deficiencies in the technique of calculation.

Prior to calculating a combination, it is essential to ask yourself, "What is the goal of this combination?" You must have a basis for evaluating the success of your analysis, and the aim of the combination must be an achievable one. The aim of the combination must always be in harmony with the evaluation of the position. It is by definition impossible, for example, that you will suddenly find a winning combination in a worse position. Use your experience and intuition to help you determine the proper aim of your combination *before* you start to calculate.

It is perfectly acceptable to correct your analysis while you are calculating. Your calculations must be in accord with your aims at all times.

For example, after calculating a combination you discover a way to win the opponent's queen, then if you have the time and energy you can calculate again and aim higher — can you give mate, too? If your new aim turns out to be unrealistic, you can always fall back on your previous calculations (since you earlier found an acceptable line).

Similarly, if your initial aim was too high, then it is necessary to lower your aim and calculate again until your aim is achievable. But don't jump around from one variation to the next. Finish calculating one line, draw a conclusion (even if it's a preliminary conclusion), and only then move on to the next variation.

It's very important not to play a move in a sharp position without any calculations to support it. A common mistake is to calculate a couple of moves and then, dissatisfied with their outcomes, to play a third move with *no* analysis behind it at all.

Sometimes it is practical to use the process of elimination, especially if you are in a position which likely has very few good moves (perhaps even a single playable move). This method starts calculating not from possible *best* moves but from the *worst* ones, with a view toward eliminating them from consideration. If you can eliminate every move as clearly losing except for one, then you really have no choice, and your decision is easy.

In determining the aim of your calculations, use your experience and intuition about which moves might be preferable or desirable. Often there will seem to be only one or two desirable moves in the position, and your task will be to determine whether they are playable.

When you begin to calculate variations, select a few moves that are worthy of consideration. We call these *candidate moves*. If you are having trouble selecting reasonable candidate moves, it may be helpful to start by considering all possible checks, captures, and other kinds of forcing moves, both for yourself and for your opponent. This will help you become properly oriented in the position.

But before you waste a lot of time and energy calculating a large number of candidate moves, determine which of them are desirable by quickly making *preliminary calculations* of only one or two moves in length. This preliminary work will set up the necessary prerequisites for successful analysis, and may also draw your attention to new moves deserving attention that were initially overlooked. Calculating variations is a dynamic process during which new moves and ideas will arise — perhaps your intended combination requires preparation, or maybe there is an in-between move that changes the situation. Discipline yourself to finish one variation and draw a conclusion before moving on to a new move or idea.

If you suffer from frequent blunders, try to follow *Blumenfeld's Rule*. After you have finished your calculations, pause for a moment to write down the intended move. Then look at the position again briefly as if you are seeing it for the first time, and ask yourself, "Does my move allow mate in one, or lose a piece?" If a quick glance at the position confirms that your intended move is not a blunder, then go ahead and play it. Applying *Blumenfeld's Rule* will save you from making many simple blunders.

Errors in calculation do not arise only because of violations of these guidelines. There are a variety of factors, mainly psychological in nature, which may also interfere with the correct assessment of the position. There are many different kinds of psychological factors, and we will present just a selection of these, illustrating them with examples. Readers can no doubt add to the list from their own experience. In what follows, we concentrate on those errors which are seen over and over at the chessboard.

Typical Psychological Errors

1. The "Impossible" Square

Very often a mistake results from improperly visualizing the chessboard and pieces. When calculating variations, you have only the current board position in front of you; consequently, some features of that position may remain in your mind even when you are visualizing a different position. Consider the following example:

Diagram 260

Ilyin-Zhenevsky – Nenarokov

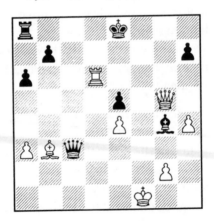

White to move

White is winning, of course. All that remains is to finish the job.

      1. Bf7+!   **Kf8**

If Black captures the bishop with 1. ... Kxf7 there follows 2. Rf6+ Ke8 3. Qg8+ Kd7 4. Qg7+ Ke8 5. Rf8 mate.

2. Qh6+?   **Kxf7**
3. Rf6+

Here White expected Black to play 3. ... Ke8, and the game would end after 4. Qf8+ Kd7 5. Qg7+ Kc8 6. Rf8 mate. But there was a horrible surprise waiting

3. ...   **Kg8!**

Suddenly it is clear that there is no mate! If White had played 2. Qxg4 (instead of 2. Qh6+) the game would have been effectively over, since then 2. ... Kxf7 would have led to mate in three (you can work that out for yourself). What happened?

The explanation is quite simple. Look at the diagram again. In the initial position the Black king cannot move to g8 for two reasons — the bishop at b3 and the queen on the g-file. During the calculating process, White subconsciously assumed that the Black king could never go there. But after 2. Qh6+ Kxf7, the bishop was gone from the board, and the queen no longer covered the g8-square, so that Black was able to use the "impossible" g8-square.

2. Disappearance of the Barrier

This is a different sort of error, but it bears some resemblance to the previous case. In this example, White decides to crack open the f-file:

Diagram 261

1. Rf1	g6
2. Qe3	Ne7

Now it seemed that nothing stood in the way of his plan, so White played ...

3. f4

... and here is what happened:

3. ...	exf4
4. Qxf4	Qxb5

White certainly did not intentionally sacrifice the piece on b5. How did this come about? The presence of a pawn at e5 had kept the possibility of ... Qxb5 out of sight and out of mind. The removal of the barrier with ... exf4 is what White missed.

3. Forgetting about a Piece

This type of mistake is a variation on the previous theme.

Alekhine-Blackburne, St. Petersburg 1914

1. e4	e5
2. Nf3	Nc6
3. Bb5	Nd4
4. Nxd4	exd4
5. 0-0	g6

6. d3	Bg7
7. f4	c6
8. Bc4	d5
9. exd5	cxd5
10. Bb5+	Kf8

Diagram 262

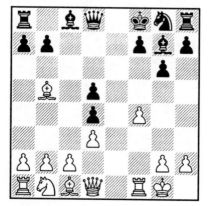

Here Alekhine played:

| 11. Nd2? | Qa5 |
| 12. a4 | |

And White lost his bishop after 12. ... a6. Alekhine later remarked, "Who can explain how such a serious oversight happened? You know, I simply forgot about the bishop. Just plain forgot that it existed!" He could take it lightly — he managed to draw the game!

Such absent-mindedness is a recurring theme at the board, often leading to some sort of catastrophe.

4. The Natural Move

A natural move is one which you count on the opponent to play as the logical and straightforward reply in the position. It is illustrated in the following position:

Diagram 263
Em. Lasker-Loman
Simultaneous exhibition, London 1913

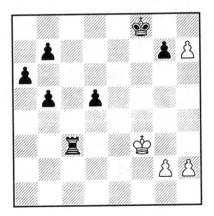

White to move

On Black's forced check of ... Rc3+, Lasker replied with the natural ...

1. Kg4?

Instead winning is 1. Ke2. An unpleasant surprise soon followed:

1. ...	Rc4+
2. Kg5	Rh4!!

Decoy.

3. Kxh4	g5+

Freeing the square of g7.

4. Kxg5	Kg7

And Black went on to win. Lasker played the obvious and logical advance to g4 but overlooked Black's sudden resource.

5. Overlooking a Counter-sacrifice

It's important to remember that the attacker is not the only one who can make a sacrifice. Sometimes the defender can save himself by unexpectedly offering to return material.

Diagram 264

Anderssen – Paulsen, Breslau 1877

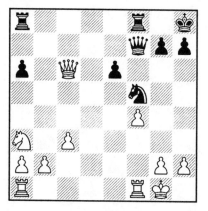

Black to move

1. ...	Qa7+

Black naturally expected 2. Rf2, but after White slid his king into the corner instead with ...

2. Kh1

Paulsen reasoned that the moment for putting the rook on f2 had passed, so he continued with the sacrifice ...

2. ...	Ng3+
3. hxg3	Rf6

Figuring that checkmate is inevitable, only to be shocked by the reply ...

4. Rf2!

This is the winning move that Black overlooked in his calculations, and it is clear why. See comments after White's second move.

6. The Danger of Success

It sometimes happens that after a player acquires a very large advantage, either in position or material, he then starts to play automatically. The result is that the advantage dissipates, with no victory in the end.

Diagram 265

Karpov – Taimanov, Leningrad 1977

In this position White has an extra pawn, plus his b-pawn is passed. Unfortunately, White starts to play carelessly.

> **1. b6?**

Better was 1. Rb1.

> **1. ...   Ra1**
> **2. Rb1**

If 2. Qe2 Qxd5 3. Rb2 Ne3!.

> **2. ...   Ng3+!**

Exploiting the overloading of White's queen.

Diagram 266

And White resigned, because after 3. hxg3 Ra8!, checkmate will occur on the h-file!

7. Unanticipated Check

Sometimes you are carrying out a plan and have considered all logical replies, but fail to take into account an unexpected check.

Diagram 267

Taimanov – Serebriisky, Leningrad 1951

Of course, in his preliminary calculations Black considered the capture on d6, but it is almost impossible to see the check on g3!

1. Bxd6!   **Rxd6**
2. Nf5!!   **gxf5**
3. Rxd6 and White won

If 3. ... Rxd6, then 4. Qg3+ (unanticipated check) 4. ... Kf7 5. Qxd6 Qb7 6. Qxc5 (with the idea of 7. Rd6) and White is winning.

Here's another example:

Diagram 268
Tal – Geller, Riga 1958

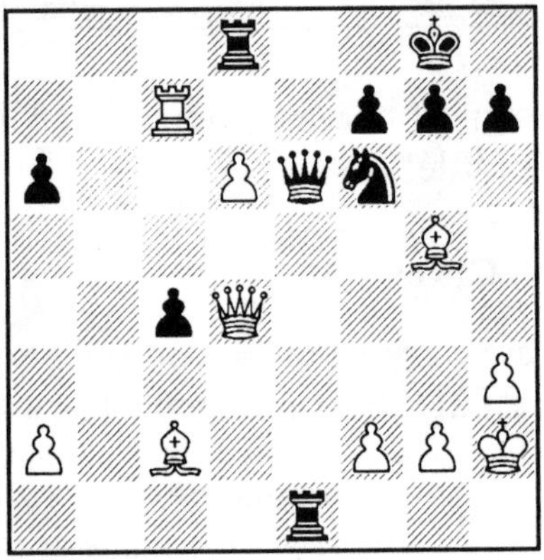

1. Bxf6

On the immediate 1. Re7 Black has 1. ... Qxe7 2. dxe7 Rxd4.

1. ...   **gxf6?**

Correct was 1. ... Qxf6 with a probable draw, *e.g.* 2. Qxf6 gxf6 3.d7 Re7 4.Bf5 c3 5.Rxc3 Rexd7 6.Bxd7 Rxd7 7.Rc6 Rd2.

2. Re7

Only now did Geller notice that he had fallen into a trap, since on 2. ... Qxe7 White would win with 3. Qg4+ — an in-between move and the unanticipated check!

Surprise Moves in the Middlegame

Let's look at another interesting example of the kind of mistake that can happen even at the highest level of chess competition.

Diagram 269
Kasparov – Petrosian, Tilburg 1981
(variation from the game)

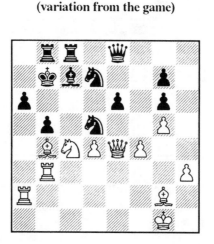

Petrosian could have played for this position where Black has an extra pawn and all his pieces are ready to help the Black king, but he sensed the danger and avoided a clever trap by Kasparov.

White wins after ...

1. Qxd5+!	exd5
2. Bxd5+	Ka7
3. Rxa6+	Kxa6
4. Ra3+	

And mate on the following move.

In the next example Tal sets a creative trap which Kasparov recognized and avoided. The variation is taken from analysis by Kasparov.

Diagram 270
Kasparov – Tal, Moscow 1983
(analysis from the game)

1. ... Nf3+ looks very strong, but it loses after White sacrifices his queen in an unexpected manner: 2. Qxf3 Qxf3 3. Na5+ Kxa8 4. Rc8 mate

Queen sacrifices are very often unexpected, and many a player has stopped his calculations after winning the opponent's queen. But winning the queen is not the same as winning the game!

Let us consider a game where Black failed to anticipate White's plan:

Diagram 271

Machulsky – M. Gurevich, Kharkov 1976

Black to move

| 1. ... | h5? |

This mistake provokes White to play a brilliant combination beginning with a queen sacrifice. Black could have avoided the combination with 1. ... Rg8 though White would still have the better game.

2. Qxe6+	fxe6
3. Bxg6+	Ke7
4. Bg5+	Nf6
5. exf6+	

Another unpleasant surprise. Black only considered 5. Bxf6+ Kd7 6. Bxd8 Kxd8 when White has two extra pawns, but Black has counterchances.

| 5. ... | Kd7 |
| 6. Ne5 mate | |

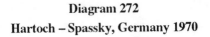

Diagram 272

Hartoch – Spassky, Germany 1970

Black to move

Black could have played the routine 1. ... Rxg2 and fallen into a trap: 2. Qf8+ Kf6 3. Qh8+ Kg5 (3. ... Ke7 4. Re1+!) and White could not play 4. Qxd4 because of 4. ... Rh2+ 5. Kg1 Rcg2 mate. But by first playing the in-between move 4. Rxf5+! (to free the f1-square for his king) White could then take Black's queen.

Instead of falling into this trap, Black played 1. ... Be8! after which White resigned, since on 2. Rg1 (there is no check on f8 now) Black wins with 2. ... Qxg1+! 3. Kxg1 Rxg2+ 4. Kh1 Rh2+ 5. Kg1 Rcg2+ 6. Kf1 Bb5+.

Diagram 273
Vidmar-Teichmann, Carlsbad 1907
(Analysis)

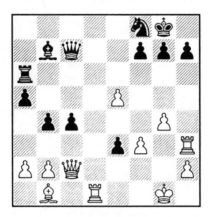

Black to move

In this position White had set a trap. If 1. ... Qxe5 there is mate in four moves with 2. Qxh7+ Nxh7 3. Rd8+ Nf8 4. Bh7+ Kh8 5. Rxf8 mate (or 4. Rh8+ Kxh8 5. Rxf8 mate).

8. The Unexpected Pin

Diagram 274

Maedler – Uhlmann, Germany 1963

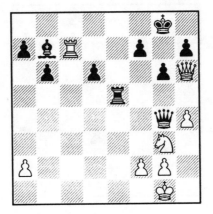

Black to move

White has just played 1. Rc7?, an attacking move which activates his rook on the seventh rank. But White overlooked a pin.

1. ...	**Re1+**
2. Kh2	**Rh1+!**
3. Kxh1	

Or 3. Nxh1 Qxg2 mate.

3. ...	**Qh3+**
4. Kg1	**Qxg2 mate**

Index

Lev Alburt

Grandmaster Lev Alburt was born in Orenburg, Russia, on August 21, 1945. For many years, he lived in Odessa, a Ukrainian city located on the Black Sea. A three-time champion of the Ukraine (1972-74), he became European Cup champion in 1976. In 1979, while in West Germany for a chess competition, he defected. Since 1979, GM Alburt has made his home in New York City.

This three-time U.S. Champion (1984, 1985 and 1990) first taught chess in the former Soviet Union under the direction of many-time world champion Mikhail Botvinnik. As a teacher, GM Alburt is at the forefront of finding new ways to teach chess to students ranging from young children to adults who wish to take up the game. *Comprehensive Chess Course* is one of the products of what is sometimes called "the new chess pedagogy."

Currently GM Alburt often conducts chess lessons by both telephone and mail — having developed course plans for both kinds of instruction. He can be reached by writing to Lev Alburt, P.O. Box 534, Gracie Station, New York, NY 10028.

"Chess is a game for life," GM Alburt says, "and that means children who learn chess not only improve their ability to reason clearly but also have a pastime that will never fail them as they grow older."

Sam Palatnik

Grandmaster Sam Palatnik was born in Odessa, Ukraine, on March 26, 1950. Odessa has given the chess world many grandmasters, including such famous names as E. Geller, V. Tukmakov, L. Alburt, V. Eingorn, K. Lerner, E. Kogan, and M. Podgaets. The name of Sam Palatnik is integral to that list.

GM Palatnik was student World Champion in 1974 and 1976, and two-time European Cup champion in 1976 and 1979. He also won the Soviet Union Championship for Young Masters in 1974, the USSR Championship and Spartakiada in 1979, and the World Open in 1991. He was awarded the Grandmaster title in 1978, and the prestigious title of "Honored Coach" in 1985. From 1985 to 1994 he was coach of the Ukrainian national teams and vice-president of the Ukrainian Chess Federation.

Since 1994, GM Palatnik has been "Grandmaster in Residence" in Nashville, Tennessee. His goal now is to help create new chess superstars in the United States.

Roman Pelts

Born in Odessa, Ukraine, on August 11, 1937, Roman Pelts holds the rank of FIDE master. Since founding the Roman Pelts Chess Studio, first in Montreal and later in Toronto, he has taught hundreds of students and is commonly regarded as Canada's top chess teacher.

In 1959, FM Pelts founded in Odessa a chess school, and among his first students were several children who later became famous grandmasters, including Lev Alburt and Sam Palatnik. FM Pelts left the former Soviet Union in 1977, taking with him the notes on which *Comprehensive Chess Course* is based.

"One of the most important teaching principles," states FM Pelts, "is to provide students only the knowledge they need at their present level of development. Give them too much, they bog down in detail; give them too little, they do not receive proper training in the basics."

243

Whether you play chess for fun or chess for blood...
Whether you're a casual player or a tournament veteran...
You're invited to join America's coast-to-coast chess club! We're the U.S. Chess Federation,
with over 85,000 members of all ages — from beginners to grandmasters!

U.S. CHESS

U.S. Chess Federation membership offers many benefits:

• The right to earn a national rating! • Big discounts on chess merchandise
• A national magazine packed with information • An official membership card
• The right to play in local, regional, and national tournaments
• The right to play officially rated chess by mail

☐**Yes!** Enroll me as follows:

☐ Adult, $40 (1 year), $75 (2 years) ☐ Senior (age 65 or older), $15/yr.
☐ Youth (age 19 or under), $15/yr. ☐ Scholastic (age 19 or under; includes bimonthly School *Mates*) $10/yr.
☐ Also, I want my FREE *Play Chess* video (a $19.95 value). I include $4.50 to cover shipping and handling costs.
☐ Send me *Play Chess I* (Covers the basics, plus winning strategic tips.)

OR ☐ *Play Chess II* (Takes beginners who know the moves all the way to their first tournament.)

Check or money order enclosed, in the amount of $_____ or charge it.
Credit card number_____ Expiration date _____
Authorized signature _____
Daytime telephone _____

Name _____
Address _____
City _____ State _____ ZIP _____
Birthdate _____ Sex _____

Call toll free: 1-800-388-KING (5464) Please mention Dept. 77 when responding.
FAX: 1-914-561-CHES(2437)   or   **Mail:** U.S. Chess Federation, Dept. 77
186 Route 9W New Windsor, NY 12553

Note: Membership dues are not refundable. Canada: Add $6/yr. for magazine postage & handling. Other foreign: Add $15/yr.